DROWNING
A COUNTY

DROWNING A COUNTY

When Urban Myths Destroy Rural Drainage

CAROL J. BOVA

For information contact:
P.O. Box 716
Mathews, VA 23109
www.insidethecrater.com

Cover and interior design by John Doppler

ISBN-13: 978-0-9907415-0-3
Library of Congress Control Number: 2014954360
First Edition: November 2014

RTP 1.03

10 9 8 7 6 5 4 3 2 1

TABLE OF CONTENTS

In Memory of My Parents

Frank and Wanda Bova

who taught me to never stop learning

1

Mathews County is Drowning

Stormwater from state roads floods yards and woodlands in Mathews County, Virginia. Mosquitoes and toxic algae flourish in the standing water in roadside ditches. Invasive reeds and cattails in flooded ditches increase the risk of excess phosphorus reaching our rivers and bays. Clogged culverts and outfall ditches obstruct the flow of streams forming swamps where none existed before. With rainwater trapped in ditches, reduced flow to waterways worsens dissolved oxygen levels resulting in impairments of the Clean Water Act.

Sea level rise or lack of elevation did not cause these negative impacts. For more than three decades, the Virginia Department of Transportation failed to provide basic drainage ditch and pipe maintenance. VDOT reduced maintenance as a response to state budget shortfalls and cutbacks, but those cutbacks became an institutional pattern supported by VDOT-created myths.

Other Commonwealth of Virginia departments oversee VDOT impacts on new construction affecting waterways. No state programs target the damage from past VDOT construction and road alterations involving stream channelization. The Code of Virginia § 33.1-69 exempts VDOT from upgrading roads to current standards, but there is no exemption from basic maintenance of a road's original drainage design and purpose.

This book contains information gathered over the past three years from observation, research and investigation. Its purpose is to explain the history and impacts of misconceptions about drainage in Mathews County and how VDOT developed its current pattern of failed, delayed and neglected drainage maintenance.

Changes in beliefs, policies and actions need to happen at local, regional and state levels to stop drowning Mathews County. Eliminating VDOT myths and sharing facts is the first step.

2

Mathews is Rural and Resilient

Mathews County is resilient. Its residents and land have survived and recovered from severe weather events over the four centuries since Europeans first arrived, as did its native population for centuries before that. Mathews County was never an urban environment, and it's improbable it will ever become one.

In part, the survival of Mathews is linked to its residents' understanding of the waters around its peninsula, its soil structure and the way stormwater drained through and across the land to numerous waterways. As Mathews grew, paths became dirt roads linking homes, wharves and churches throughout the area. Each road had ditches alongside to drain rainwater to streams, rivers or bays.

The Impact Crater Changed Mathews' Aquifers

Mathews County is one of the few occupied places in the world entirely within an impact crater. The same meteor impact that formed the Chesapeake Bay destroyed the underground formations of aquifers and confining layers found elsewhere in the Virginia Coastal Plain groundwater system. Aquifers hold water in the spaces in layers of rock and soil, and the confining layers are stone and clay between the aquifer layers that slow or stop water movement and allow water to build up in the aquifer.

Domestic wells throughout Mathews County, and in parts of Middlesex and Gloucester Counties, draw from the surficial (groundwater) aquifer or the closely associated Yorktown/Eastover aquifer. The Yorktown/Eastover connects to the surficial in many areas of Mathews County. The seasonal high groundwater level at its shallowest runs 6 to 15 inches under the surface, and the Yorktown/Eastover goes to 200 feet at its deepest level.

The impact crater deeply compressed two other aquifers in Mathews County, the Piney Point and the Potomac. The top of the Piney Point aquifer is less than 100 to 150 feet deep under West Point, but it is 400 to 500 feet deep under North in Mathews and 500 to 700 feet deep at the United States Geological Survey Bayside core-drilling site near New Point. The USGS measured the Potomac aquifer at 1905 and 2126 feet deep at the Bayside drill site. Because of these depths, neither the Piney Point nor the Potomac is used as a domestic well water source in Mathews County. The crater cut off all other aquifers found in other parts of the Middle Peninsula so they end at its rim. (McFarland and Bruce, USGS. 2006.)

How Groundwater Led to Road Construction

Groundwater levels rise and fall according to the amount of rain and snow. Water doesn't just flow down directly to pools at different levels beneath the surface. It moves downward around and between grains of sand and soil until it reaches a solid rock or clay layer with no open space, or until the open spaces are filled. When all the spaces below are filled, the water level rises. As groundwater travels eastward toward the ocean, it emerges as intermittent streams in exposed areas of lower elevations.

In Mathews, plant life draws upon the water reserves through root systems during their growing season. The US Department of Agriculture's National Resources Conservation Service (USDA-NRCS) considers the growing season as March 26 through November 12. Until trees and plants blossom in spring and start taking up water again, water uptake is greatly reduced in the dormant winter period.

Because of this pattern, there were summer and winter roads in early Mathews County. None were hard-surfaced then. "Summer" roads were a lot shorter in dry weather, but impassable in the wet season. Groundwater rose and intermittent streams flowed and crossed roads in the low spots until the groundwater level dropped with drier weather. Even "winter" roads could be turned to mud in storms.

In the 1900s, the State Highway Commission began improving these dirt roads even before the Commission began hard-surfacing roads in Mathews County in the 1920s. A volume of annual reports from the State Highway Commission to the Governor of Virginia shows that 21 miles of roads in Mathews County were maintained and drain pipes and ditches opened up in 1917. Since VDOT records show the total mileage of state roads in Mathews as 96.49 miles in July 1932, this was a considerable amount of work.

Commonwealth Transportation Board Minutes show the Virginia Department of Highways began paving the first 6.6 miles in Mathews County in December 1926 as part of a statewide plan to reduce disruptions to education and the court system. Starting on Route 38 (today's Route 198), paving was extended to Bayside (New Point) via Route 291 (now Route 14) in August 1928. The only Mathews County roads hard-surfaced prior to 1932 were these two primary roads, with the exception of one mile on what is now today's Route 660.

Before the Department of Highways built or paved roads, landowners had to provide deeded rights-of-way and drainage easements through donation or sale of land. Even though the Byrd Act created the secondary road system in 1932, all drainage ditches adjacent to roads in Mathews would have been modified by the Department of Highways in the process of hard surfacing the county's roads, especially where the Department widened and realigned roads. The one exception is for roads paved under the Rural Rustic Road program since 2002, where VDOT does not obtain additional rights-of-way. But even there, the VDOT Rural Rustic Road Program Manual says VDOT is responsible for the "reestablishment of existing associated ditches and shoulders."

Mathews Was Ahead of the Times with Biofiltration

Mathews' rural drainage system using grass-lined roadside ditches was one of the earliest methods of biofiltration and sediment transit reduction in stormwater. Residents recount cutting the grass in the ditches and on the ditch banks at least 40 years ago, and the practice probably extends much further back.

This biofiltration worked in Mathews County when more privies were still in use, and yet Mathews had fewer acres of shellfish off-limits to harvesting as shown in a 1975 Virginia Institute of Marine Science "Shoreline Situation Report". But blocked pipes, reduced ditch maintenance and cutbacks in mowing have taken their toll since then. With less fresh rainfall reaching our waterways, the water quality has declined, and we now face burdensome improvement programs under the Clean Water Act.

Mathews Was Rural in 1910—and Still Is in 2014

The 2010 population census in Mathews County showed only 46 more residents than in 1910. In 2014, Mathews has no significant industrial or agricultural contributions to runoff. The most recent U. S. Department of Agriculture county statistics from 2012 show 55 farms with 4,646 acres of land in Mathews compared to 1,387 farms with 43,205 acres in the 1910 Census of Agriculture.

The decline in water quality in the local watersheds has accelerated as the condition of the ditches has worsened and as streams channelized by VDOT have been cut off from their natural flow. Water unable to drain through flooded ditches or blocked pipes floods woodlands and adds the risk of picking up wildlife waste on the way to streams. Trees in upland woods inundated by flooding die and fall, blocking more outfalls, whether man-made or natural streams. Muck and cyanobacteria (blue-green algae) develop in standing water in the ditches. Intermittent, ephemeral and year-round streams that should carry flows from seasonal high water or rainstorms to receiving waters are dammed up behind VDOT-created berms from rotoditching or held back by blocked pipes under the roads.

The goal of urban stormwater management is to mimic pre-development hydrology. Grass-lined ditches that drain to outfalls flowing to receiving bodies of water reflect pre-development hydrology in a rural area without major pollution sources.

For an area like Mathews, with an extensive network of streams, creeks and rivers and no urban pollution, the traditional system of grass-lined roadside ditches is still a valid and reliable stormwater management system. For that system to function though, driveway pipes and culverts under roads must be open without a 50 percent or greater blockage, and roadside ditches must have a functioning outlet through outfall ditches or streams to receiving bodies of water. Where these conditions exist, there is no standing water in the ditches to allow the growth of harmful algae or to encourage invasive aquatic grasses and reeds that release phosphorus into the water as their leaves die back. Mosquitoes can't spawn without standing water, and when uplands and wetlands are not inundated by stormwater runoff from the roads, timber can flourish.

Most of the damage to the County's drainage system can be reversed with proper ditch maintenance and pipe cleaning or replacement. Improvements must be made for some channelized streams crossing under roads to allow free flow in all seasons. It will not be a quick nor an easy process, but Mathews County's infrastructure, public health and the community's welfare is at stake — and so is the health of our streams, rivers and the Chesapeake Bay.

3

Modern Myths

WHEN THOSE IN AUTHORITY REPEAT statements often enough, those statements acquire the ring of truth because they become familiar. With enough time and enough repetition, those statements take on a new life as myths that persist and are passed along within a community without challenge of their accuracy. They are the verbal equivalent of Norman Mailer's factoids:

> *Facts which have no existence before appearing in a magazine or newspaper, creations which are not so much lies as a product, to manipulate emotion in the Silent Majority. (Marilyn: A Biography by Norman Mailer, 1973. Electronic version, 2011.)*

VDOT staff repeated myths about drainage in Mathews County so often at Board of Supervisors meetings, month after month, year after year, Mathews County Supervisors and staff came to believe and repeat them. There is no way to know whether the myths were deliberately created, or if they resulted from a lack of knowledge or a misinterpretation of previous VDOT statements. After more than three decades, few employees still in the Virginia Department of Transportation system are personally aware of how roads used to drain freely through functioning roadside and outfall ditches, and most believe the myths without question.

Some of these VDOT-created myths about drainage go back twenty years or more, and some are more recent, yet each of these statements is false:

Mathews County is too flat to drain.

Ditches can't drain because of sea level rise.

If tidal ditches are cleaned, flooding will increase.

VDOT only has a few drainage easements which it is required to maintain.

Original deeds to VDOT are kept by the County Clerk at the Courthouse.

Roadside ditches weren't designed to drain completely.

VDOT has only a 30-ft prescriptive easement on secondary roads in Mathews.

Stormwater trapped in ditches has no impact on roadbed integrity.

Ditch work can only be done in winter after leaves have fallen from the trees.

Perhaps the most damaging myth for the well-being of the county and its drainage is the one that says, "Mathews County is too flat to drain." Looking at a statement made to the Mathews County Board of Supervisors by Don Wagner, Virginia Department of Transportation Resident Engineer, may help show why this belief is so widespread today.

> *Mathews County cannot adequately drain because of its flat*
> *topography as evidenced by a U.S. Army Corps of Engineers study*
> *some years ago. (Board Minutes, Sept. 29, 1992.)*

Although this sounds reasonable on the surface, there is no Corps of Engineers statement that the area cannot drain. The US Army Corps of Engineers 1960 Hurricane Survey of Garden Creek does say the Garden Creek area is relatively low and flat with a maximum elevation of 10 feet above mean sea level. "The land slope is generally in an easterly direction with the maximum slope of about 5 feet per mile."

This 1960 work was done after a 1956 Hurricane Survey had recommended further study for the Garden Creek area, and it included both field investigations and office studies. It was presented to Congress as "...a Report, Together with Accompanying Papers and Illustrations, on an Interim Hurricane Survey of Garden Creek, Mathews, County, Virginia." (House Document No. 216, 88th Congress, 2nd Session, 1964.) The Corps of Engineers coordinated the study with the Department of Highways and the US Fish and Wildlife Service.

> *(The Department of Highways provided)...the estimates of costs*
> *for highway alterations for several plans considered. Topographic*
> *survey and tide frequency data developed during the investigation*
> *were furnished to the Department of Highways for use in future*

development of the highway system and for operations during
periods of tidal flooding.

The 1960 Corps of Engineers survey did find that a combination of low earth levees, road revisions and tide gates would prevent tidal flooding from hurricanes or nor'easters with tides less than 7 feet above mean sea level. This conclusion was based on the twin hurricanes of 1933, with similar storms expected to occur once in 75 years. (Hurricane Isabel 70 years later in 2003 was the next equivalent storm.)

The cost of the suggested levees and tide gates would have been $979,000. (The 2014 equivalent is $7.84 million.) Mathews County would have been responsible for 30% of that amount.

2% in lands and damages
17% in road revisions
11% in project costs

Annual charges to the County would have been $48,000 in 1960 ($384,441 in 2014). The County was unable to cover these expenses, and the project went no further.

Although the county could not afford the local share of the cost of the levees and tide gates, two recommendations could have been implemented. The failure to act on one of them, "preserving and rehabilitating the barrier beach," led to an event with serious repercussions for drainage in Mathews County—the breach in the barrier beach from Chesapeake Bay to Winter Harbor.

4

The Breach in Winter Harbor

From Lost Beach to Failing Watershed

Hurricanes cause massive displacements of sand. They can change beaches and islands and cut new channels in days. But for shorelines affected by wave action reaching the shore at certain angles, sand also moves in a slower process called longshore transport. This wave action erodes barrier islands and beaches unless an adequate supply of sand replenishes the material moved away by the waves.

Wave action affected the Garden Creek watershed and moved sand southward along the coastline of the Chesapeake Bay. This movement of volumes of sand, known as littoral drift, is why people could picnic on sandbars along the shore at New Point near the Lighthouse at the turn of the century and occasionally through the following century. Betsy Ripley, a Mathews resident, described playing at New Point over fifty years ago on dunes one week and returning the next to find them gone and new ones further south.

In 1978, waves from an April nor'easter cut through the barrier beach, opening Winter Harbor to the Chesapeake Bay. This breach in the barrier beach caused a failure in the Garden Creek watershed drainage system which impacted 10 square miles of Mathews County. The 1980 Shore Engineering "Drainage Study of the Garden Creek Area" shows this drainage area runs from the Chesapeake Bay 2-1/2 miles west to the VDOT stormwater storage ditches behind the convalescent center at Mathews Main Street and Tabernacle Road (Route 611).

Movement of sand and sediments through wave action was not well understood until the 1950s, and research increased through the 1970s to the present. Today, we are experiencing the problems caused by actions taken, or not taken, 70 to 80 years ago.

Storms Changed the Mathews Coastline

The April 6, 1889 Nor'easter, several others in the 1800s and the August and September 1933 hurricanes impacted patterns of sand transport and reshaped the Mathews County coastline along the Chesapeake Bay. The jetties at Garden Creek prevented the movement of sand southward from along the coast down to the barrier beach at Winter Harbor from 1933-34 through the 1940s. The Corps of Engineers 1960 Hurricane Survey of Garden Creek describes how the construction of that channel interfered with the southward movement of sand which instead collected along the jetties, and later, in the navigation channel itself.

*A project to provide a navigation Channel and drainage
improvement was constructed by the Civil Works Administration
and the Federal Emergency Relief Administration during 1933
and 1934. The channel located at the mouth of Garden Creek,
was 30 feet wide and 4 feet deep and was protected by pine pile
and sheet pile jetties extending 600 feet across the beach into the
bay. Damage by storms, deterioration of the jetties, and shoaling
reduced the channel to a point that it was no longer usable
for navigation by 1940. Within a few years, the channel was
completely closed to drainage.*

In addition to the impact of the jetties, large quantities of sand
were removed from Haven Beach in the 1940s for building roads
according to the 1962 United States Department of Agriculture
Soil Survey of Mathews County. Anecdotal reports from Mathews
residents say that sand was taken for building construction as well.

There may be no way of determining whether the breach in
the Winter Harbor barrier beach after the April 15, 1978 nor'easter
was inevitable, or if it could have been prevented by the beach
replenishment recommended by the Corps of Engineers in their
1960 Garden Creek report. Since more than 11% of Mathews
County's land is affected by the Garden Creek watershed drainage
failure, perhaps the idea of restoring the breached barrier beach
should be revisited in the context of pre-disaster storm mitigation
by Mathews County, FEMA, the Army Corps of Engineers and the
Virginia Institute of Marine Science (VIMS).

Some dune and beach restoration has already taken place south
of the breach where the Corps of Engineers has placed dredge spoils
as directed by VIMS. Other barrier beach restorations have been
completed or are underway in coastal areas from Massachusetts
to Florida and Louisiana, so there is ample experience on how to
accomplish it here if funding can be identified.

When Two Myths Connect

Barrier island and barrier beach erosion and loss is usually swept into the sea level rise category without acknowledging the impacts of storms and wave energy or insufficient sand for aggradation (rebuilding the barrier islands through the depositing of sediment). And so the fate of the barrier islands and beaches in Mathews County connects to another myth.

Myth: Ditches in Mathews can't drain because of sea level rise

The National Oceanic and Atmospheric Administration— NOAA—has no tide gauges near the 210 miles of shoreline waters of Mathews County, and yet drainage issues in the County are dismissed by VDOT as being caused by sea level rise on one hand and the belief that the county is too flat to drain on the other.

If sea level rise were intruding on the lowest ditches adjacent to the marshes, the flooded ditches on the upland side of the roads would be filled with salt water, but freshwater plants and animals living in them show this is not the case. Rainwater accumulates in the upland-side ditches because blocked pipes and obstructions in the ditches prevent movement to the downhill saltwater side of the road and drainage through the marsh.

Beyond the presence of freshwater in the upland ditches, there's even stronger evidence: if the county were too flat to drain, tidal ditches in the lowest elevations could not empty to bare sand and mud at low tide twice a day as far inland as they have for the past one hundred years or more. Since the tidal ditch banks aren't overtopped by high tides twice daily, neither relative sea level rise nor lack of elevation is the problem—blocked pipes and obstructed ditches are. So how did the myth, "Sea level rise prevents proper drainage," develop?

Relative sea level rise is occurring at increased rates in other areas of the Chesapeake Bay. Using Dorchester County, Maryland on the east side of the upper Chesapeake Bay as an example, more than half of that county is between 2 and 4.9 feet. (Sea Level Rise: Technical Guidance for Dorchester County, Maryland. 2008.)

The Dorchester County tide gauge over a 64-year range has shown an increase of 3.48 mm per year of local sea level rise, and the Dorchester marshes have saltwater inundation and loss of vegetation from the flooding.

Mathews County's Numbers Tell a Different Story

The 2013 FEMA Flood Information Portal for Region III used recent LIDAR (Light Detection and Ranging) measurements to update Mathews County's elevations and flood risks. The new map shows the lowest areas of Mathews County are in the 5 to 7 feet range. The 2013 FEMA Preliminary Coastal Study also used the LIDAR mapping, and the new analysis shows Mathews County with 0.1 to 2.0 feet less storm surge along the shore than did previous reports. If local sea level rise had significantly affected Mathews County, the storm surge would have been modeled at a higher, not lower, level.

Relative Sea Level Rise Is Local and Mathews County Has No Tide Gauges

Without tide gauge readings over an extended time for Mathews County waters, estimates for sea level rise in Mathews have been based on readings from NOAA tide gauges as far away as Lewisetta and Colonial Beach on the Potomac River and Sewall's Point near Norfolk, south of the Chesapeake Bay. (MPPDC, Initiating

Adaptation Public Policy Development, 2012.) None of those gauges are within the Chesapeake Bay Impact Crater.

With no gauges in Mobjack Bay, the North River, the East River, the Piankatank River or the Chesapeake Bay adjacent to Mathews County, there is no way to determine if readings for Mathews would be higher or lower. Formerly, the closest gauge was on the York River at Gloucester Point before Hurricane Isabel destroyed it. Its replacement is also on the York River at the Coast Guard Training Center in Yorktown. Another gauge in Kiptopeke on the Eastern Shore across the Chesapeake Bay is within the crater.

The mean sea level rise in Mathews cannot be estimated from the tide gauges in Norfolk, Lewisetta or other locations as Table 1 illustrates. These readings demonstrate that mean sea level rise in one area, even if relatively close in distance, cannot be used to determine the level in another. Relative sea level rise is a local condition and not directly connected to another location's sea level rise trend.

Wetlands Watch supplied sea level rise information to the Middle Peninsula Planning District and Mathews County officials based on experience in the Norfolk area at Sewell's Point, one of the areas with a higher MSL (Mean Sea Level) trend. One major difference between Mathews County and Norfolk though, the population in Norfolk was 67,452 in 1910 and 242,803 in 2010.

Massive amounts of groundwater removal in Norfolk result in land subsidence, making relative sea level rise higher as well. The City of Norfolk's website states that their Water Department "serves approximately 850,000 people with treated water and handles wastewater for approximately 240,000."

Table 1.

NOAA Tide Gauge Location	Distance from	in miles	Approx. miles from Winter Harbor, Mathews County	Mean sea level trend (mm/yr)	Variance (+/- mm/yr)
Philadelphia, PA	Chesapeake City	55	not on Chesapeake Bay	2.79	0.021
Chesapeake City, MD (Chesapeake Delaware Canal)	Philadelphia	55	NE 172	3.78	1.56
Duck, NC	Oregon Inlet	27	SE 70	4.59	0.94
Oregon Inlet Marina, NC	Duck	27	SE 97	2.82	1.76
Lewisetta, VA	Colonial Beach	32	NE 43	4.97	1.04
Colonial Beach, VA	Lewisetta	32	NE 80	4.78	1.21
Kiptopeke, VA	Lewisetta	67	SE 24	3.48	0.42
Sewall's Point (Norfolk), VA	Kiptopeke	23	S 29	4.44	0.27
Gloucester Point, VA (to 2003)			SW 20	3.81	0.47

Major Conclusions
Land subsidence and global sea-level rise combine to cause
relative sea-level rise in the southern Chesapeake Bay region.
Land subsidence causes more than half of the observed relative
sea-level rise. Aquifer-system compaction causes more than half
of the land subsidence. (Eggleston, USGS Circular 1932, 2013.)

The City of Norfolk's experience of 242,803 people in 54 square miles should not be used as a model for Mathews County because the population in Mathews was 8,922 in 1910 and 8,968 in 2010, in 86 square miles. Greatly decreased livestock numbers offset possible increased modern household uses of groundwater. There is no heavy industry in Mathews, and domestic water is drawn from wells mostly in the surficial aquifer or the adjoining Yorktown/Eastover aquifer. Because fewer than 200 residential units in Mathews are on the Hampton Roads Forced Sewer Transmission line, most household wastewater is returned to the ground via septic systems, eliminating water drawdown as a cause of subsidence.

With the low population density of 104 persons per square mile compared to nearly 4,500 in Norfolk, Mathews has minimal watershed impacts—except for VDOT's roads, blocked ditches, pipes and outfalls.

Lighthouse Changes Don't Prove Dramatic Sea Level Rise

Another Wetlands Watch argument for sea level rise in Mathews County is the change in conditions around the New Point Comfort Lighthouse between 1885 and the present. If sea level rise were responsible for the increased stretch of water between the shore and the lighthouse, there should have been a corresponding increase in the depth of water next to what would have become submerged landforms. NOAA navigation charts from 1872 and 2009 show this did not happen.

All depth notations on the following two charts are in feet at mean low water. The 1872 chart uses fathoms to depict depths beyond 18 feet. (One fathom is equal to six feet.) Areas with depths beyond 18 feet are shown as undotted on the 1872 chart and are outside the detailed area shown here. The 2009 chart uses feet for all notations. For example, on the 2009 chart, there is a notation of 19 feet. On the full 1872 chart, that general location shows 3 1/2 to 3 3/4 fathoms or 21 to 22.5 feet.

Historical documentation prepared for the Mathews County Historical Society by Candace Clifford shows that the New Point Comfort Lighthouse was completed in 1805, and by 1814, erosion of a sandbar turned the lighthouse peninsula into an island. By 1839, further movement of sand made a boat necessary for the lighthouse keeper to reach the mainland. The 2008 site assessment for the Lighthouse by C.S. Hardaway, Virginia Institute of Marine Science, confirmed longshore transport (wave action moving sand and sediment) was responsible for the breach in the Deep Creek barrier beach that left the Lighthouse on its current island.

Navigation Chart of the Chesapeake Bay, 1872

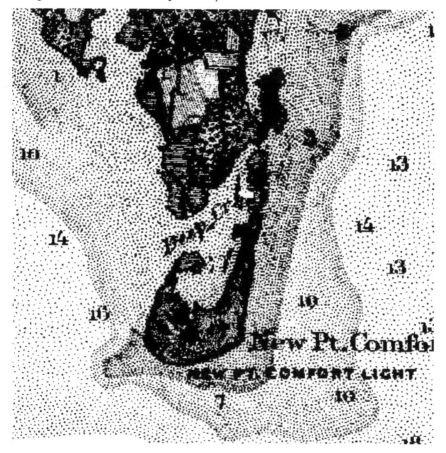

Images from NOAA's Office of Coast Survey Historical Map & Chart Collection courtesy of the National Oceanic and Atmospheric Administration (NOAA), Office of Coast Survey.

Nautical Chart 12238

Chesapeake Bay, Mobjack Bay and York River Entrance, 2009

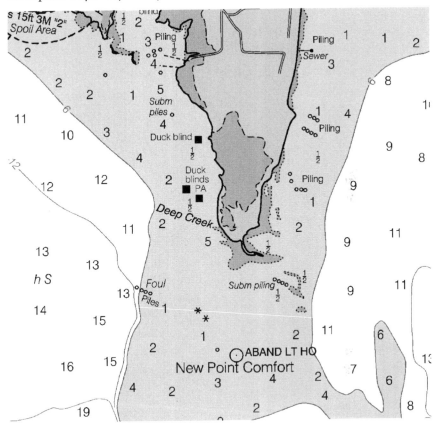

Images from NOAA's Office of Coast Survey Historical Map & Chart Collection courtesy of the National Oceanic and Atmospheric Administration (NOAA), Office of Coast Survey.

Extreme Sea Level Rise Models Don't Match Reality in Mathews

The Middle Peninsula Planning District Commission uses two sea level rise reports with extreme estimates which also cannot be used for Mathews County because their models do not accurately depict conditions in or around the county. One is from the National Wildlife Federation, and the other is from the Chesapeake Bay Program.

The much higher sea level predictions from the National Wildlife Federation's 2008 technical report, "Sea Level Rise and Coastal Habitats in the Chesapeake Bay Region," estimates a 27.2 inch increase by 2100 and refers to "Mobjack Bay, Hampton."

> *This site encompasses the upper tidewater region of Virginia from the mouth of the Piankatank River and Mobjack Bay down to Hampton.*

The 2008 National Wildlife Federation report starts with average global sea level rise, rather than relative sea level rise and applies its computation to the entire Chesapeake Bay region from Maryland to Virginia Beach. Table 1 shows how local sea level rise can be very different from one point to another when actually measured by tide gauges, Lewisetta's 4.97 mm/yr to Kiptopeke's 3.48 as an example. Using the global sea level rise average is like taking the global average of human male height and applying that number to a small local population. The global number cannot be taken as an accurate picture of heights in the small locality unless confirming measurements are made.

The initial starting conditions in the National Wildlife Federation report are questionable as well. Because most of Mathews County has less than 25% impervious land in any given area, it is considered "undeveloped" and therefore, "unprotected from sea-level rise," ignoring homes which have been elevated or constructed on higher ground, but don't have extensive hardscaping. (Hardscaping is land covered by impervious paving or structures that prevent water from filtering down through the soil.)

Although the NWF report acknowledges it was completed prior to the FEMA LIDAR mapping of the region and uses older topographic maps which show a lower elevation than the new FEMA mapping does, the report is wrong. It treats areas with a 10 to 20 foot elevation range the same as areas with 4 to 6 feet elevation and claims that .39 meters (1.27 feet) of sea level rise by 2100 will turn most of Mathews into swamps. The new swamp areas depicted include areas that never flooded in Hurricane Isabel's 7 to 8 ft storm surge or any other storm. The author's own property is shown as becoming as swamp, but it has a 10.5 ft elevation certificate, has never flooded since it was built in 1957 and is in the unshaded Zone X of the FEMA Floodplain Map, meaning it is outside the 500-year flood plain.

Other Mathews areas on the NWF image are at least 20 ft in elevation and not near rivers or creeks. So even though 15-inches may be reasonable at the upper range of sea level rise estimates, the forecasted impacts are not. Unless there is additional barrier beach or barrier island loss, 15-inches of sea level rise will not inundate any part of Mathews County, not even the lowest marshes.

Most of the areas predicted to become swamps on the NWF report with a 15-inch rise in sea level by 2100 are shown on the Mathews County Comprehensive Plan as non-tidal wetlands. Many of these "wetlands" are actually uplands flooded by failed sections of the VDOT drainage system, but the only way to prove that fact is to restore the drainage system and allow the natural upland vegetation to re-emerge.

Doubling Sea Level Rise Estimates to Allow for Errors

The Chesapeake Bay Program's 2008 report, "Climate Change and the Chesapeake Bay" begins with the National Oceanic and Atmospheric Administration 2001 Technical Report (NOS CO-OPS 36) "Sea Level Variations of the United States 1854-1999," by Chris Zervas:

> *Sea-level rise during the second half of the 20th century has been monitored accurately at six sites in the Bay, ranging from 2.7 to 4.5 mm yr with an average of 3.5 mm/yr.*

The 2008 Chesapeake Bay Program report, however, then adds an additional estimate to allow "for errors in the climate-projections and in the semi-empirical sea-level-rise model," resulting in an estimated increase of 27.6 to 62.99 inches by 2100.

This addition to the estimate isn't based on evidence from tide gauges or measurable changes in actual conditions—it's a mathematical maneuver proposed by Stefan Rahmstorf in 2007. Two other groups of scientists responding in *Science* magazine, September 28, 2007 disagreed with the methodology.

> *Although we agree that there is considerable uncertainty in the prediction of future sea-level rise, this approach does not meaningfully contribute to quantifying that uncertainty. (Schmith et al. 2007; Jevrekeva et al. 2007)*

Another technical comment by Schmith, Johansen and Thejll suggested other statistical methods might be more appropriate.

The point of a model should be to reflect reality, not invent an alternate one. Rejecting this addition to the estimate is not saying that there is no relative sea level rise in Mathews County waters. The point is, no one can say with any certainty what the amount of rise is, or has been locally. It is likely that post-glacial land subsidence (isostatic rebound) and other factors have led to a moderate rate of as much as 3 to 3.8 mm per year here, which would amount to 12 to 15 inches in a century. (This is comparable to the NWF estimate of 1.27 feet or 15.24 inches by 2100. It is their conclusion about the impact of that increase that is incorrect.)

What's Wrong with Reasonable Estimates Based on Real Readings?

While it would certainly be more accurate to have actual tide gauge readings for Mathews County, there are none. Even using the 3.5 mm per year average from 2013 to 2050 of the six Chesapeake Bay sites in the Zervas 2009 "NOAA Technical Report NOS CO-OPS 053, 1854-2006 Sea Level Variations" report, results in an estimated increase of 5 inches by 2050 and an additional 7 inches by 2100. It is possible, however, the rate of sea level rise has been and will continue to be lower for Mathews County, especially since our marshes are not inundated on a daily basis like those in Dorchester County, Maryland with its recorded sea level rise of 3.48 mm per year. It is unlikely, given the condition of marshes in Mathews, that the local rate of sea level rise has been higher, or Mathews would be seeing its marshes submerged like those in Dorchester County.

EPA on Winter Harbor's Marshes and Sea Level Rise

Marshes also line tributaries and the landward facing sides of Winter Harbor, the mouth of Strutts [sic] Creek, just south of Gwynn's Island, and the southern bank of the Piankatank.... The marsh areas are expected to accrete sufficient sediment to only keep pace marginally with a 2 mm per year increase above

current sea level rise rates, and are likely to be lost with a 7 mm
per year rate increase. (Titus and Strange. 2008.)

If stormwater drainage from the roads to receiving bodies of water is maintained, the marshes in Mathews County identified in the EPA report can adapt to local increases in mean sea level. The marshes will keep pace as long as relative sea level rise doesn't exceed 7 mm per year, an amount twice that expected using the information in the 2009 Zervas report.

5

Back to the Breach

How MPPDC Report Errors Lead to Wrong Conclusions

Based on the 2001 or the 2009 NOAA reports by Zervas, the probable increase in local sea level for Mathews is 5 inches by 2050, and more likely, less. MPPDC chose to use extreme estimates that are 2.4 times that level, grossly inflating the economic impact of sea level rise.

> *Using available topographic data, MPPDC staff generated county maps to assess the economic and ecological impacts of 1 ft sea level rise by 2050 for select vulnerable areas within each county. The assessment revealed that approximately $187,005,132.10 - $249,451,074.50 worth of infrastructure (i.e. roads, houses, onsite disposal systems, etc) and wetland function may be impacted and/or lost by sea level rise. (Middle Peninsula Climate Change Adaptation I. MPPDC, 2009.)*

"Onemo and Diggs: 2000 Current" (top); "Onemo and Diggs: 2050 Impact" (bottom). Adapted from MPPDC 2009 report.

Onemo and Diggs map used courtesy of Middle Peninsula Planning District Commission.

More troubling than the higher sea level rise estimate is the use of obsolete maps in the 2009 MPPDC report, and the fact the MPPDC 2000 map view does not show the breach across the barrier beach into Winter Harbor that occurred after the April 1978 Nor'easter. Even the 2050 map used to quantify the infrastructure that would be lost to sea level rise in Onemo and Diggs in Mathews County doesn't reflect the same breach in the barrier beach caused by wave and wind action in 1978.

MPPDC's 2009 report, "Assessing the economic and ecological imparts of sea level rise for select vulnerable locations," again used the inaccurate maps to illustrate the impact of sea level rise in Mathews County.

The Virginia Institute of Marine Science documented the Winter Harbor breach in their Mathews County Shoreline Management reports in a series of aerial photographs and diagrams comparing shoreline changes in Mathews from 1937 through 2002. "Shoreline Evolution Chesapeake Bay and Piankatank River Shorelines" (Hardaway, 2005) is also online and discusses the breach in the Winter Harbor barrier beach. The changes are shown in aerial photographs from 1937, 1953, 1968, 1982 and 2002.

The omission of the Winter Harbor breach is such a major error, it invalidates the entire MPPDC sea level rise assessment for Mathews County. This raises a question about the oversight of reports produced using NOAA grants administered by the Virginia Coastal Zone Management Program at the Department of Environmental Quality.

The Virginia Coastal Zone Management Program Missed MPPDC Map Errors

The Virginia Coastal Zone Management (CZM) Program is a network of Virginia state agencies and local governments, established in 1986 through an Executive Order, which administers enforceable laws, regulations and policies that protect our coastal resources and foster sustainable development. (DEQ Coastal Zone Management Website)

In 2001, CZM started on a project that developed into the Virginia Coastal Geospatial and Educational Mapping System (GEMS). As a Commonwealth agency involved with coastal mapping, CZM should have been aware of the error in the MPPDC maps which were based on a 1965 topographic map created before the breach occurred. As previously noted, VIMS, who works closely with CZM, has tracked and published the changes in the Mathews shoreline between 1937 and the date of each VIMS shoreline inventory. These publications were readily available to Commonwealth agencies, including CZM. But CZM accepted the 2009 and subsequent MPPDC reports with the mapping errors.

The incorrect MPPDC report information was disseminated as part of MPPDC presentations given across the state. Some of these presentations and attendees are listed in the MPPDC Phase 3 Climate Change report, *Initiating Adaptation Public Policy Development.*

a. The Impact of Climate Change on Water Resources and Water Infrastructure: Mitigation and Adaptation workshop (11/15/2010). Graduate students, VTech professors, representatives of the water industry and county governments and planners.

b. Virginia Coastal Partners Workshop (12/7/2010). A workshop of stakeholders (Planning District Commissions, Virginia

Institute of Marine Science, Virginia Commonwealth University,
Department of Game and Inland Fisheries, Virginia Department
of Conservation and Recreation, etc.) involved in Tidewater
Virginia Coastal Management to share projects that assist in
the overall management of the Virginia coastline (i.e. fisheries,
land-use, shoreline management, green infrastructure, etc).

c. VTech Field Trip: Climate Change and Sea Level Rise
Adaptation in the Middle Peninsula (3/16/2011). MPPDC staff
hosted a field trip of Virginia Tech graduate and undergraduate
students to the region.

d. Lunch and Learn Program with the Chesapeake Bay Board of
Realtors (4/6/2011).

e. Middle Peninsula Realtors (6/15/2011) - Coordinated a
speaking engagement with the Middle Peninsula Realtors
Association. "As this real estate community is the gate keeper to
new residents moving into the Middle Peninsula, they are able to
share this information and local issues that may be pertinent for
potential buyers."

f. Mid-Atlantic Marine Educators Association Conference
(11/08/2011). "MPPDC staff presented the current impacts of
climate change and sea level rise identified within the Middle
Peninsula."

The incorrect information and conclusions shared with so
many influential individuals, including decision-makers at the
Virginia Department of Transportation, can only lead to a new
myth seemingly supported by the MPPDC studies implying it is too

expensive to invest in maintenance of roads that will be lost to sea level rise.

Misleading Example Bolsters a New Myth

MPPDC has also used misleading information to reinforce a premise. An example is the MPPDC slide about sea level rise impacts on roads in Gloucester County in the MPPDC Phase 3 Climate Change Report. The presentation of the slide show in that report is available on the Virginia DEQ Coastal Zone Management website under, "Reports and Publications, 2010 Virginia Coastal Partners Workshop Presentations."

What's Local Governments' Role in Climate Change?— Lewie Lawrence, Middle Peninsula Planning District Commission

Abstract: Although climate change is a global phenomenon, local strategies to adapt and plan for climate changes will be important to protect public safety, health and welfare of Middle Peninsula residents. Climate change and sea level rise remains a very unsettled issue amongst Middle Peninsula constituents and local elected officials. Learn how the coconut telegraph and a rural belief system impacts climate change policy development at the local level.

A dramatic image of a house in a flooded marsh with water over a road in front of it bears the wetlandswatch.org watermark. The image was taken from the Wanda D. Cole photograph on the front cover of the report, "Technical Guidance for Dorchester County," prepared in 2008 for the Maryland Department of Natural Resources. The photo was manipulated to elongate and reduce the height of the image, which created the effect of a longer, lower building in a flatter terrain than in the original, perhaps to give a better impression of a Gloucester County location. (The actual location of the image is not identified in the presentation.)

The text on the slide is next to a map of southeastern Gloucester County (the Naxera and Guinea areas used in the first MPPDC Sea Level Rise Assessment report of the Climate Change Adaptation report).

- *Raise 1/2 mile of road 10 inches - $320,000*
  (no permits and environmental cost)

- *18% of Gloucester Area VDOT*
  Secondary Road Budget

  Putting it into perspective:
  $320,000 = 1/2 mile of road
  $640,000 = 1 mile of road
  $32,409,600 = 50.64 miles of road
  (amount of road in snapshot to right)

But there is no mention of the fact that the 1/2 mile road segment crosses the flood plain of the Whittaker Creek headwaters. Is the flooded road problem on Route 614 (The Corduroy) really related to sea level rise? Is the water level elevated in the adjacent marshes as it is in the image of Dorchester, Maryland? If not, did anyone investigate whether the pipes under the Gloucester road are adequate to carry the natural watershed flow from the upper marshes along the headwaters to Whittaker Creek during storm events? Should the road have been built in its present location, or should there have been a bridge over the headwater marsh area in the first place?

There are no answers in the report or the presentation. Only the broad-based assumption sea level rise is the cause and how much it might cost to raise this road and all the other roads in that portion of Gloucester County. It would have to be inferred as well, that the same conditions apply in Mathews County, even if complete facts might indicate otherwise.

MPPDC Bias Mocks Mathews' "Coconut Telegraph and Rural Belief System"

When local residents on the Mathews County Planning Commission challenged the data MPPDC presented, MPPDC did not take them seriously. Instead, the report dismissed the challenges, even though the comments on the local nature of sea level rise were accurate, and MPPDC's "scientific data" was theoretical and not based on actual conditions in Mathews or on any tide gauge measurements.

> *Providing scientific data to support or disprove a parochial position on the issue carried little influence and was generally dismissed as not being geographically relevant to Mathews County: "data from the York River and not Mathews Specific, followed by… that's New Point data, not East River data." (Middle Peninsula Climate Change Adaptation, Phase 2)*

This MPPDC attitude was carried forward in the previously listed PowerPoint presentations with a slide mocking residents labeled, "The Coconut Telegraph." A toddler about 3 years old speaking into a tin-can phone tells a grey-haired woman, "I hear that sea level rise is fake!" ("What's Local Governments [sic] Role in Climate Change?" MPPDC 2010.)

The presentation goes on to use Wetlands Watch photographs; the first clearly shows the area around the New Point Comfort Lighthouse was a barrier island/beach complex and also shows a proposed subdivision plat to develop the area in 1904.

What the slide doesn't share is The New Point Comfort Corporation planned to build a resort near the New Point Comfort Lighthouse by filling in the marshes and building up the beaches. Basically, they planned to create something that didn't exist at the time the map was drawn. The Mathews County deed book for 1904/05 shows a few lots were sold, but not enough to carry out the plan, and the company went out of business.

The next slide says, "TODAY- 5 ft water covers more than 1,000 plated [sic] subdivision lots," above a photo showing open water between the lighthouse and the shore with the caption, "shoreline has moved 1/2 mile 1885." This is a misleading combination of information. First, most of the lots never existed because the marshes weren't filled in, and next, because barrier beaches and barrier islands are subject to change by wind and tides as discussed earlier in this book. Barrier beaches and islands gain sand; they lose sand. A comment in the *Daily Press* newspaper demonstrates this.

> As long ago as 1814, a local businessman noted that the New Point Comfort Lighthouse was in a poor location, as "the water already washes its base." (Judith Haynes, Daily Press, May 15, 2002.)

This statement was made nine years after the lighthouse was built. So the fact that the beaches grew between 1814 and 1885, and then were lost as a result of hurricanes and wind and wave action in the 1900s, does not point to sea level rise. A yellow banner across the slide with the open water and lighthouse, capitalized in yellow, says, "THIS PROVES NOTHING!!" Although intended as further mockery, it actually makes a true statement.

MPPDC Doesn't Have a Sterling Record for Accuracy

Inaccurate information from MPPDC again entered the public domain with the 2011 Regional Water Supply Plan. MPPDC used obsolete details about Middle Peninsula aquifers from 1977 State Water Control Board charts, which were also used in 2002 in "Water Supply Management on the Middle Peninsula of Virginia— An Information Review."

According to the 1977 chart, the "Yorktown Aquifer has low yield potential. Principal and upper artesian aquifers are not suitable for potable use (high chlorides)." Yet in 2006, USGS hydrologist Randy McFarland reported, "The Yorktown-Eastover aquifer is the second most heavily used source of groundwater in the Virginia Coastal Plain." (USGS PP1731.)

Why the discrepancy in the 1977 report? Written prior to the 1984 discovery that Mathews County is entirely within a meteor impact crater, the 1977 authors were unaware Mathews aquifers do not follow the typical pattern seen elsewhere in the Atlantic Coastal Plain. A news release from the United States Geological Survey on November 13, 2013 states that the salt-water from the North Atlantic Ocean was trapped in pockets between rocks as a result of the meteor impact that created a hole 56 miles wide. This trapped brine is twice as salty as today's seawater, but no one knew in 1977 that it might have affected areas of fresh water also trapped under the rubble by the impact.

Again illustrating how misinformation enters into general use, Mathews County's 2030 Comprehensive Plan, adopted in January 2011, used the obsolete 1977 statement from MPPDC.

Much of the residential and small commercial water supply of the County is provided by private wells that draw water from the shallow, near surface "surficial" aquifer, sometimes referred to as the water table aquifer.... This aquifer has a low potential for water yields and is high in chlorides and minerals, affecting its quality as a potable water source.

The Comprehensive Plan gives the source of its information as the Middle Peninsula Planning District Commission, "Water Supply Management on the Middle Peninsula of Virginia—An Information Review"; 2002.

The primary source of domestic well water in Mathews County is, however, the Yorktown-Eastover aquifer, as well as the frequently adjoining (i.e., connected) surficial aquifer. Only two other aquifers exist in Mathews County, and both are far below the level of drilled domestic wells in the county: the top of the Piney Point aquifer is about 350 to 500 ft below the surface, and the top of the Potomac aquifer is about 800 to 1800 feet below the surface (McFarland, 2006.)

Obsolete MPPDC Information Taints Economic Development Strategy

MPPDC used the 1977 State Water Control Board report in the 2013 Middle Peninsula Comprehensive Economic Development Strategy (CEDS) in connection with the Middle Peninsula becoming part of the expanded Eastern Virginia Groundwater Management Area (EVGMA). MPPDC Executive Director Lewis Lawrence explained, "We use the 1977 report because it was/is the most current for some information needed." But the Yorktown/ Eastover aquifer, one of the main domestic water sources in Mathews County, is not listed under Table 3, Aquifers of the Middle Peninsula. The Yorktown/Eastover is listed on an inset on the following page in Figure 10, which used the obsolete 1977 information.

While Mathews County isn't looking for big industrial development, smaller businesses are justifiably concerned about an adequate water supply. Obsolete and incorrect negative information is not a draw for new business.

How Thirty-Year-Old Information Could Have Helped MPPDC's Reports

Considering the fact MPPDC said their mapping efforts involved VIMS, it's hard to understand how the breach in Winter Harbor was overlooked in the MPPDC sea level rise scenario.

Mapping efforts completed by the MPPDC in collaboration with the Virginia Institute of Marine Science (VIMS) are derived from best available digital elevation models (DEM) using USGS contours between 5 and 10 feet.

Even without the VIMS knowledge base, if MPPDC hadn't lost track of the 1980 Shore Engineering Garden Creek drainage study, now cited as one of the "1980's Major MPPDC Accomplishments," the authors of the MPPDC climate change and sea level rise assessment reports and presentations might have come to different conclusions. Perhaps they also would have recognized the validity of Mathews Planning Commission members' objections to the sea level rise assessment presentation and refrained from insulting mockery in state-wide presentations.

Setting that aside, the Shore Engineering study offers some of the most accurate information available about the VDOT drainage system in the Garden Creek Watershed, one that used to handle 11 percent of the County's drainage before the breach in the beach occurred.

6

Tracking Down Lost Records

In 2013, the MPPDC staff could not locate the 1980 Shore Engineering Garden Creek drainage study*, and it didn't turn up in a search of the MPPDC library of documents at their Saluda office. (*In 2014, the MPPDC website lists the study as "Mathews County Drainage Project.")

However, the 1980 MPPDC minutes book contained copies of correspondence referring to the Garden Creek drainage study and provided the name of the winning bidder for the contract, Shore Engineering. With the specific date and study title, Mathews County Director of Planning and Zoning John Shaw located a copy in the County's old files.

The report indicates Shore Engineering was unable to find an economically feasible solution for the 1978 breach in Winter Harbor's barrier beach. This breach, as previously discussed, changed the hydrology of Winter Harbor and Garden Creek and destroyed most of Garden Creek's drainage capability for ten square miles of the county. But the Shore Engineering report did offer specific comments and recommendations.

Based on the conclusions reached in the analysis, the following recommendations are made:

1. Clean and maintain existing ditches, culverts and drainage ways.

2. After the existing drainage system is cleaned, if the land above elevation 5 (5 feet above MSL) still does not drain, the system should be checked for grade to determine specific high points and to determine the flow capacity of various drainage channels. The results of the grade and capacity check should then be used to design and construct a drainage system which will assure drainage of land 5 feet above MSL or higher.

Had the MPPDC sea level rise assessment report and presentations incorporated the Shore Engineering recommendations, it would have resulted in a very different calculation of infrastructure that could be lost to sea level rise. Land above 5 feet can drain, even with sea level rise at the current rate—if the VDOT drainage system is functioning. The elevation of all land in the Garden Creek watershed, other than in the marshes, is 5 feet or higher.

1980 Mathews Supervisors Request Drainage Equipment to Drain VDOT Ditches

In October 1980, after reviewing the Garden Creek drainage study, a Mathews County Board of Supervisors resolution said, in part:

*WHEREAS, the Virginia Department of Highways and
Transportation constructs and maintains roads in Mathews
County which, by their existence, contribute to the drainage
problems of private landowners of Mathews County; and*

*WHEREAS, it is in the best interest of the Virginia Department of
Highways that roads in Mathews County be drained as efficiently
and effectively as possible.*

*NOW, THEREFORE, BE IT RESOLVED that we, the Mathews
County Board of Supervisors, do hereby request additional funds
for drainage work in Mathews County, specifically funds for
drainage equipment which would assist local highway department
personnel in draining the highway ditches in Mathews County.*

This never happened. There was no concentrated effort to clean ditches or open pipes in the study area. Some pipes and ditches have been addressed in the past 30 years after specific requests from county supervisors or residents, but others are in the same or worse condition as in 1980.

One example is a property with frequent flooding at the corner of Bethel Beach Road (Route 609) and Old Garden Creek Road (Route 610) because the roadside ditches won't drain. A 12" cross pipe under the road at that intersection was shown as completely blocked on the 1980 drainage study. Inspection of the pipe shows it was still blocked in 2013. Because the land is higher on the opposite side of the road, there are no cross pipes to convey water away from the property owner's side of the road until after a hard 90 degree turn going toward Bethel Beach. At that point, in front of a large cedar tree, there is a cross pipe meant to take water across the road and out to the marsh. But it is so blocked, that water can only move in the top 2-3" of the pipe. On the other side, the pipe opening is completely underwater because the roadside ditch is obstructed.

Further toward Bethel Beach, this same roadside ditch is at a lower elevation, but empties with each tide because it is clear of obstructions. All it would take to restore this section from the corner of 609 and 610 to the clear ditch is cleaning the ditch and cleaning the pipes. Yet VDOT has not acted since the Saluda Resident Engineer Sean Trapani and the Fredericksburg District Administrator Quintin Elliott saw this area on a tour with G.C. Morrow and Carol Bova in March 2013 and promised action. Since the pipe-cleaning truck has been observed repeatedly since then in Gloucester and Middlesex Counties, it appears the VDOT Saluda Residency has no immediate plans to address the 609 pipes. Isn't 34 years long enough to wait for a response?

2014 USGS National Map Errors Connect to a 1980 Report

Maps from the 1980 Shore Engineering study go beyond the immediate Garden Creek area watershed and show major ditches connecting to creeks in some adjacent areas. A section of one of the 1980 study maps shows the headwaters of Put In Creek and parts of Morris Creek and the ditches that connected to them from Main Street as well as areas further north—in 1980.

These same lines were shown on the historical USGS topographic maps in 1965, and those ditches functioned at that time. But the 2011 USGS topographic map was generated by a computer-mapping program and not land-verified. Some historical elements from earlier maps, including ditches, were picked up. The problem is some of those old ditches in Mathews County no longer exist, and others no longer function, even though they are still in the 2014 National Map.

Before the new Liberty Square Courthouse on Buckley Hall Road was built, ditches existed at the rear and sides of the former school property to carry stormwater to Put In Creek. These ditches were partially destroyed by the construction and replaced by retention ponds. Now nothing flows towards Put In Creek because of the damage from the new Courthouse construction. Some water moves across Buckley Hall Road to an outfall intended to go to Morris Creek, but that outfall is blocked before reaching Morris Creek, and water accumulates in the woods, damaging timber crops.

The Hyco Subdivision lies to the north of the Main Street and Buckley Hall Road intersection. At least two major drainage outfall ditches to Morris Creek on the north and east perimeters of the Hyco Subdivision were destroyed by either construction of the subdivision or the Mathews County sanitary system lines.

Phantom Images of Former Ditches Used In VDOT Engineering Plans for Mathews

One now-destroyed ditch that used to be on the north perimeter of the Hyco Subdivision was mislabeled as Put In Creek on state and federal mapping programs. VDOT treated this and other destroyed ditches as still functioning in computations for engineering decisions on the new Mathews Route 14 Main Street Drainage Improvement Project. As a result, the plans have water running uphill south toward Put In Creek, and two cross pipes under Buckley Hall Road are to be replaced by four larger ones, even though one of the existing pipes has had a utility pole through the middle of it for years, and neither had been cleaned in decades. VDOT plans to obtain the rights-of-way for the four larger pipes are still underway in June 2014, even though VDOT staff had been advised of the mapping errors at the public hearing in December 2012. Detailed comments explaining the mapping errors and how they occurred were sent as a public hearing comment by email on December 24, 2012. No response was ever received, and the Main Street Drainage Improvement Plan was scheduled to be funded for construction in 2015.

Why the National Map Is Wrong About Mathews

State and federal agencies share responsibility for the National Hydrography Dataset (NHD) maintenance and accuracy, but major changes in the Chesapeake Bay shoreline in 1978 that affected drainage in the Garden Creek watershed aren't reflected in the NHD. No one on the state level has addressed the historical artifacts that still show up on the computer-generated state and federal maps like the ditch mislabeled as Put In Creek.

Perhaps this helps to explain why no one in the Commonwealth's Coastal Zone Management Program recognized map errors used by MPPDC to calculate losses expected from sea level rise in Onemo and Diggs. Extrapolation of loss estimates from maps not showing the existing breach in the Winter Harbor barrier beach not only misleads local government officials and planners, it does not reflect the actual state of the marshes today.

If we look again at the mission of the Coastal Zone Management Program, another question is how can they regulate and protect what they can't correctly identify?

> *The Virginia Coastal Zone Management (CZM) Program is a network of Virginia state agencies and local governments, established in 1986 through an Executive Order, which administers enforceable laws, regulations and policies that protect our coastal resources and foster sustainable development. (http:// www.deq.virginia.gov/Programs/CoastalZonemanagement.aspx)*

The National Hydrography Dataset

The NHD interconnects and uniquely identifies the stream segments or reaches that make up the Nation's surface water drainage system. The NHD is a national framework for spatial position for surface water features, their attribution, their connectivity in a flow network….(USGS-VGIN Memorandum of Understanding)

Virginia has identified the NHD as a significant GIS component to support regional cooperative initiatives, effective and cooperative land management, cooperative ecosystem management, and a myriad of other applications. Thus it is included as an essential geospatial dataset in the Virginia Spatial Data Infrastructure.

The United States Geological Survey has suffered budget cutbacks that forced them to use computer-generated mapping instead of the time-intensive land-verified mapping of the past. Errors between different programs and analysis of aerial photography are inevitable, so a system was set up for the individual states to participate in correcting and updating their portion of the National Map.

Virginia's principal steward is VGIN, the Virginia Geographic Information Network. Their role is to coordinate stewardship activities and be a point of contact to accept and review edits and forward them to the USGS. They are responsible for stewardship of fifty Hydrologic Units in Virginia. (Mathews is in Hydrologic Unit 02080110—Great Wicomico-Piankatank.)

VGIN works on the NHD stewardship in cooperation with the Departments of Forestry (DOF), Environmental Quality (DEQ), Conservation and Recreation (DCR), Game and Inland Fisheries (VDGIF) and Virginia Institute of Marine Science (VIMS).

Why Didn't the Six Responsible Commonwealth Agencies Act?

Both parties of this MOU recognize that maintaining NHD consistency, currency, and accuracy will benefit both parties and all users of the NHD.

Each of the Commonwealth entities involved in the NHD stewardship has had activity in Mathews County, but there seems to be no record of any of them attempting to correct the NHD to reflect changes that happened in 1978 and the 1960s. Other maps, such as FEMA's street-view of the Mathews County, VA Flood Information Portal, have the same errors in the Chesapeake Bay shoreline as the NHD.

NOTE: In July 2014, the USGS accepted a Ditches of Mathews County project request by Carol J. Bova to correct the flow lines for Garden Creek and the Winter Harbor barrier beach breach. The USGS said the shoreline errors related to changes in the topographic map sections will be corrected at the next three year review. The USGS assistance is greatly appreciated.

Non-Technical Bottom Line

The Virginia agencies responsible for correcting and updating the NHD haven't corrected the problems that result in faulty GIS maps used by the County, the MPPDC and VDOT. All three entities believe the Commonwealth's GIS-maps are accurate. The GIS maps are probably used in some way by every Commonwealth agency, and there is no way to estimate the long-term cost of map errors.

7

From Heavy Equipment
to Shovels and Rakes

VDOT on the Importance of Drainage

The VDOT Board of Supervisors Manual's stated purpose "is to provide new members of the Board of Supervisors, or other public officials, with a better understanding of the Department."

The manual makes a strong statement about the importance of drainage maintenance:

> *Adequate drainage conveyances and facilities are integral components of a safe and structurally sound roadway infrastructure. Inadequate or improperly maintained drainage facilities are responsible for most pavement failures and soil erosion. A road may have its serviceability seriously curtailed, or may even be made impassable as a result of improper drainage*

maintenance, or inadequate facilities. One of the most important duties of maintenance personnel is the repair and maintenance of the highway drainage system and the importance of this activity cannot be over-emphasized.

Drainage Easements Acquired by the Department

The Department assumes full maintenance responsibility within the limits of the drainage easement. (Board of Supervisors Manual, 2012)

VDOT not only failed to provide maintenance for drainage easements in Mathews County, they tried to shift their responsibility to the County. It took sixteen years, but they succeeded—using delay, misleading statements and reframing the purpose of the County's contributions through revenue sharing. VDOT's failure to track easements deeded to VDOT for drainage and drainage maintenance completed the attempt to shift responsibility.

How Three Years of Revenue Sharing Turned into Sixteen

How did a VDOT suggestion to apply for a $50,000 revenue sharing match from the state to hire heavy equipment for a one-year outfall cleaning project become sixteen years for three "one-year" revenue sharing projects totaling $201,076? How did hiring heavy equipment turn into inmate labor and local VDOT crews using shovels and rakes?

The minutes of the Mathews Board of Supervisors tell the story—and it's a long drawn-out story that was difficult to boil down. All quotes are from the minutes for the month shown unless otherwise identified.

Don Wagner, VDOT Resident Engineer (Saluda), came before the Mathews Board of Supervisors on August 25, 1992. Heavy rains in the first half of the month had caused flooding over a number of roadways, and he blamed:

> ...the inordinate amount of rainfall, development along roadways which increase runoff, low elevations and little contour characteristic of much of the County's land.

He failed to mention the neglected condition of the ditches prior to the August rains. When one supervisor brought up outfall ditches needing maintenance work, Don Wagner agreed it was a problem.

> Due to a lack of machinery and employees and, in some instances, property owner permission, the Department has been unable to keep them clean of obstructions.

(Note here and later, Mr. Wagner never says it was not VDOT's responsibility to maintain the outfall ditches between roadside ditches and receiving bodies of water.)

After discussion, the Board approved a resolution to be sent to the Commissioner of Transportation stating in part:

> Due to limitations in state manpower, equipment and/or funding resources, many drainage ditches, particularly outfall ditches, have not been adequately maintained.

This 1992 request mirrored the previously mentioned one made by the Mathews supervisors to the Commonwealth Transportation Board in October 1980.

...that the Virginia Department of Transportation allocate additional manpower, equipment and/or funding resources as necessary to adequately maintain existing roadside and outfall stormwater drainage ditches and other storm water facilities in Mathews County and to install such new ditches and facilities as deemed necessary to improve the stormwater drainage system in the County.

The Origin of the VDOT "Too Flat to Drain" Myth

In September 1992, Don Wagner stated that VDOT had kept the roads clear and well-drained for the past five years, but changed his statement slightly from the previous month.

Mathews County cannot adequately drain because of its flat topography as evidenced by a U. S. Army Corps of Engineers study some years ago.

A powerful statement, except it wasn't true.

The Army Corps of Engineers study never said Mathews cannot drain because its topography is flat. Their 1960 Hurricane Survey stated the Garden Creek area is relatively low and flat with a maximum elevation of 10 feet above mean sea level. "The land slope is generally in an easterly direction with the maximum slopes of about 5 feet per mile."

The Corps of Engineers did make three recommendations:

- raise the road elevations in the area as high as practicable commensurate with other requirements

- improve the drainage system, and

- encourage the preservation and rehabilitation of the barrier beach along the Chesapeake Bay.

VDOT ignored the recommendations from the Corps of Engineers' study as well as the Shore Engineering study 20 years later.

Introduction to Revenue Sharing

Don Wagner came to the Board of Supervisors in March 1993 and offered to report back on revenue sharing "for ditch maintenance and other drainage improvements" if the County was interested in matching the state funds. In April, he brought a proposal for "improvement and maintenance of outfall drainage ditches." He said the work would either be performed by rented equipment or contracted. The Board approved up to $50,000 in matching funds and prepared a list of outfall ditches:

PRIORITIZED LIST OF ELIGIBLE PROJECTS FOR REVENUE SHARING PROGRAM, FISCAL YEAR 1993-94 MATHEWS COUNTY

Clearing outfall ditches at the following locations (see attached map)*:

1. *From Route 633 to Edwards Creek, parallel to and northwest of Route 636.*
2. *From Route 630 to Route 631, parallel to and north of Route 198.*
3. *From Route 644 to Route 613, parallel to and southwest of Route 611.*
4. *From Route 619 northeast to Route 660.*
5. *From Route 639 to Stutts Creek, parallel to and east of Route 696.*
6. *From Route 618 northwest to Route 617.*

7. *From Route 617 to North River, between Route 618 and Route 619.*

8. *From Route 637 to Barn Creek, parallel to and northeast of Route 680.*

9. *From Beaverlett to Garden Creek, parallel to and north of Route 610.*

10. *From Route 608 to Horn Harbor, parallel to and east of Route 607.*

*no map in Board Minutes book

On April 29, 1993, the *Daily Press* quoted Don Wagner as saying:

We've taken basically the ones that give the roads the greatest problem...Some of these ditches are a half-mile or a mile long that we're going to have to go in and clean out in order to make sure that we can keep the water flowing and away from the roads.

Don Wagner told the Board at the June 22, 1993 meeting that $42,300 was approved for revenue sharing by the state and should be available in July. Work was to begin in August.

On July 28, 1993, the Daily Press reported:

...the money will be used to hire equipment to clear a 12 to 15-foot wide swath along the ditches...Some of the ditches have not been cleaned for decades.

In August, the Board learned project funds were allocated for October, and at the October 21 meeting, Larry Dickerson, VDOT Acting Resident Engineer (Saluda), told the Board work had begun on the first ditch off Route 639. Supervisor Charles Ingram requested financial statements after three ditches were completed.

On January 25, 1994, Larry Dickerson reported two outfall ditches had been completed off Route 639 in Redart and 633 on Gwynn's Island.

> *The Route 633 ditch took two days to complete using shovels and rakes. An itemized expense sheet will be furnished to the Board as soon as it is finalized. The Route 639 ditch took one day to complete at a cost of $575.*

On February 22, 1994, an 11th ditch added for Route 681 in Hallieford.

> *Responding to a question from Mr. Vail about the drainage problem on Route 681, Mr. Dickerson stated that there will be revenue sharing funds left over from the current drainage improvements project and this money will be used to improve drainage.*

Additional Funding of $75,000 From 1994-2000 Six-Year Plan

The Mathews County Secondary Highway Construction Six-Year Plan had drain pipes on Sheet #1 under Incidental Items at $25,000 in 1994-95 and $10,000 in each of the subsequent five years. (This amount is not carried forward as part of the revenue sharing records.)

June 28, 1994: Woody Woodward, VDOT Resident Engineer (Saluda), reported to the Board:

*Initially 10 ditches were identified that needed more than
the routine cleaning. Of the 10 original ditches, 5 have been
completed with over 9,000 feet of ditching completed by hand by
local VDOT crews.*

*Nineteen ditches have now been identified as needing work...
(Woody Woodward) advised the Board that he hopes to have at
least 10 ditches completed within the next two months and try to
have all 19 completed by winter. He stated that to do the job in
the correct manner, it needs to be done with equipment and not
with manpower utilizing shovels.*

The Board of Supervisors failed to point out this was the exact
reason the County entered into a revenue-sharing agreement in
March of 1993. Nor did they question why VDOT failed to use
the necessary equipment or if the work done had been adequate to
restore the outfall ditch functions.

End of Year One: 1993-94 Revenue Sharing Project, June 30, 1994

*$42,300 allocated from the State and $42,300 from the County.
Starting Balance: $84,600
Spent: $6,000.
Balance available: $78,600.*

By September 1994, three months into Year Two, the first 11 ditches
had been completed at a cost to date of $27,089. Most had been done
by hand, because no plan had been established to remove trees that
had been growing in and next to the ditches for 20 years or more.

End of Year Two: 1993-94 Revenue Sharing Project, June 30, 1995

Starting Balance: $78,600.
Spent: $21,089.
Balance available: $57,511.

August 22, 1995: Woody Woodward, VDOT Resident Engineer (Saluda).

> *Chairman Ingram advised Mr. Woodward that the*
> *Transportation Safety Commission has identified 45 ditches*
> *in the County that are in need of drainage improvements. The*
> *Commission has prioritized them by grouping them in 5 groups*
> *with the first group being the highest priority.*

VDOT's New Myth: Ditch Work Should Be Done After Leaves Have Fallen

September 26, 1995: Larry Dickerson, VDOT Assistant Resident Engineer (Saluda).

> *In response to a question from Chairman Ingram, Mr. Dickerson*
> *stated that VDOT has not yet received the priority listing of*
> *ditches which are being recommended for maintenance by the*
> *Transportation Safety Commission. He noted that after VDOT*
> *receives the list it will set up a meeting with County officials and*
> *set limits as to how much work can be done and at what cost the*
> *contract preparation will take place. That process normally takes*
> *2-3 months. By that time, it's spring and that is not a good time*

to start work on outfall ditches due to plant growth. Therefore the work will more than likely not be done until next winter.

October 24, 1995. Woody Woodward, VDOT Resident Engineer (Saluda):

Due to the delay in receiving a prioritized list of ditches, it will likely be next fall before the actual work is undertaken because there is only $50,000 available to do the work and it is less expensive to accomplish the work after the leaves and foliage have fallen from the trees and bushes.

Woody Woodward's statement in October 1995 marks the beginning of VDOT's practice of doing ditch work in the winter. There are obvious flaws in this concept, but the practice has become the standard in Mathews County.

Why Ditch Work Should Not Be Done in Winter

1. The official USDA growing season in Mathews County is March 26 through November 12. Plants do not actively take up water from the ground between mid-November and near the end of March—leaving more water in blocked ditches.

2. There is minimal evaporation from ditches during the winter.

3. Working saturated soil leads to more erosion and sediment movement.

4. Reseeding must be done in the growing season. Bare soil leads to more erosion.

5. The slope of ditches cannot be determined while they are flooded.

6. When plants and saplings are not removed from ditches in the growing season; saplings become trees; shrubs and the roots and rhizomes of perennial plants continue growing the following spring; the combination perpetuates the problem of obstruction from plant growth.

Second Revenue Sharing Project—1996-97

February 27, 1996. Woody Woodward, VDOT Resident Engineer (Saluda) discussed revenue sharing with the Board of Supervisors.

> *This program allows the Department to match state funds with*
> *local funds for the construction, maintenance or improvement*
> *of highways and other transportation-related facilities. He*
> *noted that this program could be used for the improvement and*
> *maintenance of outfall drainage ditches which would enhance*
> *transportation safety and would reduce public (i.e., roadway) and*
> *private property damage arising from ponding stormwaters.*

The Board passed a resolution to participate in a revenue sharing project again in the amount of $50,000 for fiscal year 1996-97.

June 25, 1996. Frank A. Pleva, Mathews County Administrator:

> *...advised the Board that revenue sharing money has been*
> *awarded in the amount of $35,890 and, combined with funds*
> *previously set aside by the Board of Supervisors, brings the total*

amount of funds available for drainage ditch maintenance to
approximately $100,000 from both state and local sources. He
reported that priority one ditch work should begin in the Fall of
1996.

End of Year Three: 1993-94 Revenue Sharing Project, June 30, 1996

No further reported progress.
No financial updates.
Last reported balance: $57,511.

How the County Responded

The Board of Supervisors again failed to question VDOT on the lack of progress. They did not demand an exact accounting of the previously funded project, and they accepted the new myth that work couldn't be done until the winter, even though generations of local farmers had maintained their ditches successfully in the dry seasons. The Board put up another $35,890 of County funds.

July 1, 1996—1993-94 and 1996-97 Revenue Sharing Projects

Prior Balance: $57,511.
$35,890 from the State and $35,890 from the County added.
Combined Starting Balance: $129,291.

July 23, 1996. Woody Woodward, VDOT Resident Engineer (Saluda), reported to the Board meeting about the 45 outfall ditches identified in August 1995 as needing work.

There are fourteen (14) #1 priority ditches that remain on
the project list after review by VDOT officials including
environmental review staff. Five (5) ditches were deleted from the
list due to environmental restrictions or other reasons.

The next day, July 24, 1996, the *Daily Press* reported that this
work would be finished by April (1997), but there was no mention
of the other 26 ditches identified in August 1995 in the news or at
Board meetings in the previous year.

When Heavy Equipment Became Unskilled Manual Labor

October 22, 1996. Chris McDonald, VDOT Assistant Resident
Engineer (Saluda):

...advised the Mathews County Board of Supervisors that only
one (1) bid was received for the Outfall Ditch Maintenance
project and this bid was excessively high.

December 17, 1996. Woody Woodward, VDOT Resident
Engineer (Saluda), and David Harmon, Superintendent of the
Middle Peninsula Regional Security Facility (Jail), discussed using
inmates for ditch work.

Mr. Harmon stated...there are no restrictions regarding locations
the inmates can work and they can use shovels, chain saws and
bush axes. He advised the Board that he can provide as many as
15 inmates or as few as 7-8.

Mr. Harmon stated that the ratio of supervisors to inmates is
1-8. Mr. Woodward stated that a representative from VDOT can
be on site and, depending upon staff availability, he can have a

VDOT representative for 2 crews of 4 inmates each. He noted that the work will involve shoveling, removing debris and beaver dams.

Inmates removing debris using shovels, chain saws and bush axes was not the heavy equipment VDOT told the Board of Supervisors was needed in 1993 for ditches not cleaned in decades.

April 22, 1997. Woody Woodward, VDOT Resident Engineer (Saluda).

Mr. Woodward reported that all of the Priority I ditches have been cleaned by inmates from the Regional Security Center. He noted that additional work is required on some of the ditches once the water level in the ditches goes down. He further reported that VDOT staff has done some complementary outfall ditch work...

Approximately $12,000 has been spent on this project. Mr. Woodward advised the Board of Supervisors that there are eleven (11) Priority 2 ditches, three (3) of which require special permits. Adjacent property owner research has been completed, letters are being generated to obtain permission to clean the ditches and environmental reviews have been completed. work can be initiated as soon as the security center inmates are available. Mr. Woodward reported that he has discussed the possibility of contracting the work on some of the ditches that require machinery to clean them and agreed that it would be done on an "as needed" basis. Mr. Woodward stated that the ditch cleaning project is not expensive as it is being done now with the assistance of inmate labor.

End of Year Four: 1993-94 and 1996-97 Revenue Sharing Projects, June 30, 1997

Fourteen Priority I ditches cleaned by inmates, with some needing additional work after the water went down. No one reported in the Board minutes if this occurred.

Combined Starting Balance: $129,291.
Spent: "Approximately $12,000."
Balance: $117,291.

No supervisor commented that all Priority 1 ditches required heavy equipment and were done instead by inmate manual labor. No one asked if the inmate labor had been effective. Neither the County supervisors nor VDOT staff seemed to recall VDOT Resident Engineer Don Wagner's comment to the *Daily Press* in April 1993:

> *About all we've been able to do with the forces and the money*
> *we've got is go in there and hand-clean these outfall ditches,*
> *working through the woods as best we can, and you really can't*
> *do what needs to be done by hand-cleaning.*

July 22, 1997. Woody Woodward, VDOT Resident Engineer (Saluda).

> *Mr. Woodward further reported that the cleaning of ditches has*
> *slowed down this summer but is expected to increase this fall.*

November 21, 2000. Edward F. Smyth, Jr., Assistant County Administrator:

*...gave a brief update on the Drainage Ditch Program, noting
that the list of priorities has been approved by the Transportation
Safety Commission. He also noted that additional nominations
for ditch work county-wide would be sought from citizens.*

December 19, 2000. Jamie Surface, VDOT Assistant Resident
Engineer (Saluda), "reported that four ditches have been cleaned so
far this season."

January 18, 2001. Glenn McMillan, VDOT, "filling in" while
hiring is completed for three positions in the Saluda Residency
"informed the Board of several drainage ditches that are currently
being cleaned and maintained."

End of Years Five through Eight: 1993-94 and 1996-97
Revenue Sharing Projects

June 30, 1998 through June 30, 2001
Starting Balance: Approximately $117,291 left in June, 1997.
Amount Spent: Unknown.
Balance: Unknown.

The records fell silent about amounts spent on the 1993-94 and
1996-97 outfall projects during these years. No details of total
locations or number of ditches worked on were provided.

October 23, 2001. Edward F. Smyth, Jr., Assistant County
Administrator:

Mr. Smyth informed the Board that the ditch maintenance program will begin sometime in December 2001 and end mid-March 2002. He also noted that the items at the beginning of the list marked with "A" priority will be completed first as these ditches have not been maintained in 10 years or more.

Four ditches were marked as Priority 1-A. (See Table 2.)

- From Hyco Corner through woods to High School along Critter Lane

- Mathews High School

- State Route 647 (Lovers Lane) just beyond end state maintenance on left and right to Morris Creek

- Onemo

February 26, 2002. Marcie Parker, VDOT Resident Engineer (Saluda).

Ms. Parker informed the Board that she has received a list of 37 outfall ditches that need maintenance throughout the county. She stated that 12 of those have been completed so far. Ms. Parker expects all 37 ditches will be completed by the end of March 2002.

Table 2.

	Transportation Safety Commission 2001 Outfall Ditch Priority List		
Priority	Applicant	Location	Community
1	John Blake	SR 660 SE of SR 687 - outfall ditch to un-named creek to the East River	Cardinal
1	David Shuber	Garden Creek area - SR 613 (Knights Woods Rd) through woods to Garden Creek	Diggs
1	Charles Richardson	North side SR614 (Williams Wharf Rd) along West side of Christ Church to Church Creek of East River	Mathews
1	Elaine Owens	SR613 (Callis Field Rd) to Garden Creek Canal between properties	Mathews
1	James Guy	SR684 (Gayle Ln) near end of state maintenance on left to Put In Creek	Mathews
1	Charles Lirette	SR653 1 mile North of Holly Point Rd to Stutts Creek	Mathews
1	Virginia Love	600 ft South of SR 708 & along East side SR 642 to cove off Billips Creek	Moon
1	Florence Rainier	SR657 West under SR14 to Morgan's Branch North end	North
1	Ken Kurkowski		North
1	Judy Burroughs	2000 Application - SR14 to SR714 to Horn Harbor - south end of SR714	Susan
2	Rita Cannon	From SR 198 to Chapel Creek (map attached)	Cobbs Creek

2	Jefferson Starke	1st right off SR681 in Cow Neck to Hills Bay	Hallieford
2	Deborah Daniels	St. Ives Ct. - runs behind Cricket Hill apartments & adjacent business area	Mathews
2	George Gayle	SR621 (Glebe Rd) to SR 684 (Gayle Ln) to Put In Creek	Mathews
2	James Abrams	SR 641 (Pine Hall Rd) East to SR 647 (Lovers Ln) to Morris Creek	Mathews
2	James Abrams	From SR 647 to Morris Creek (see application)	Mathews
2	Richard Couch	From junction of SR 621 & 684 to Put In Creek (map attached	Mathews
2	Aubrey Brown	From SR 14 to Horn Harbor	Port Haywood
3	Frank Monaghan	Between SR 629 & 630 to roadside ditch along SR630 to Outfall Ditch to Piankatank River	Cobbs Creek
3	Anthony Tanner	SR 740 roadside ditch to outfall ditch beyond Pickle property Unknown water body	Gwynn
3	Jane L Smith	.4 mi on SR 637 (Gwynnville Rd) on left to Barn Creek	Gwynn
3	William DeLoatch	SR198 @ Forrest Ln running West to Queens Creek (map attached)	Hudgins

3	Raymond Mountford	SR 611 (Courthouse Rd) along private lane to East River	Mathews
3	Earl Morag	SR 14 south 3d lane past Beulah church (adjacent owner refused to submit)	New Point
3	Susan McCreary	SR617 south side along Green Mansion driveway to Green Mansion Cove	North
3	Louies Lane	SR 702 off 609 to Winter Harbor	Onemo
1A	Mary White	From Hyco Corner through woods to H.S along Critter Ln. (map attached)	Mathews
1A	Mathews High School		Mathews
1A	Shannon Wheeler	SR647 (Lovers Ln) just beyond end state maintenance on left & right to Morris Creek	Mathews
1A	Ray Hudgins		Onemo

End of Years Nine and Ten: 1993-94 and 1996-97 Revenue Sharing Projects, June 30, 2002 through June 30, 2003

No financial reporting in Board Minutes since 1997.

March 26, 2004. Neena Putt, Mathews County Supervisor. Alfred Harris, VDOT Supervisor (Mathews).

> *Mrs. Putt asked about the outfall ditch program and Mr. Harris stated that no outfall ditches were completed from this year's applications. The inmate program was cut due to budget reductions at the state level.*

This comment by Mr. Harris overlooks the revenue sharing funds still being held from 1993-94 and 1996-97. The County Administrator and Supervisors did not mention that amount either.

End of Year Eleven: 1993-94 and 1996-97 Revenue Sharing Projects, June 30, 2004

No financial reports in Board Minutes during the previous year.

VDOT Transfers Responsibility to Mathews County

November 23, 2004. Marcie Parker, VDOT Resident Engineer (Saluda).

> *Ms. Parker explained that there remains $60,538.17 in Revenue-Sharing Funds for Mathews County that have never been expended. She stated that these funds include county funds and the VDOT match which were set aside approximately 10 years earlier and never expended. Her suggestion to the Board was to create a countywide outfall ditch program, transferring the*

money to that newly created program.... Ms. Parker explained that VDOT would start with the list that Mathews County has compiled on outfall ditches. The existence of the revenue-sharing money will make it possible to hire contractors to complete a certain amount of work. She noted that inmates will also be used as much as possible, although new laws have made the use of inmates for such work much more difficult.

The Mathews County Board of Supervisors voted 5-0-0... to approve a resolution to authorize the transfer of the approximately $60,538.17 in Revenue-Sharing Funds into a new account for a countywide outfall ditch cleaning program for Mathews County.

It took VDOT ten years, but they succeeded in transferring responsibility to Mathews County for outfall maintenance—even for those outfall ditches where VDOT held easements.

VDOT's Misleading Statements to the Commonwealth Transportation Board

At the June 16, 2005 meeting of the Commonwealth Transportation Board, the FY05 Supplemental Allocation of revenue sharing funds was questioned by CTB member Hanley.

Prior to approval Ms. Hanley asked if these ever ran out, some of the reallocations are from 1993 and 1994.

Mr. Estes responded that this is a result of the reconciliation of completed projects that had small dollar amounts on them so they are now being pulled up to a new project.

Ms. Hanley asked if we (VDOT) now had a process to close these projects out sooner.

Mr. Estes responded that yes we do, we are making strides in our reconciliation efforts. (http://www.ctb.virginia.gov/resources/ June_minutes.pdf)

Mr. Estes' claim that $60,538 was the result of "small dollar amounts" from completed projects doesn't make sense, especially since the heavy equipment and operators that money was supposed to fund were never obtained. There may have been some incidental use of rented equipment, but it was never described in any Board minutes between 1993 and the 2005 CTB meeting. Apparently nothing more was spent until 2006, when a third revenue sharing project began because the available balance is identical to the new account balance in November 2004.

End of Years Twelve and Thirteen: 1993-94 and 1996-97 Revenue Sharing Projects

June 30, 2005 through June 30, 2006

Last Reported Balance (June 30, 1997)	Approx. $117,291.
Amount Spent July 1, 1997 to June 30 , 2006	$56,752.83
Subtotal	$105,234.17
Balance June 30, 2006	$60,538.17

August 31, 2005
Commonwealth Transportation Board
FY06 Revenue Sharing Allocation to County of Mathews
Project 9999-057-146, N501 UPC 77415, Drainage Improvements

State: $22,348
Locality: $22,348

October 24, 2006. Steve Whiteway, Mathews County Administrator.

> *The county has signed a revenue sharing agreement with VDOT*
> *whereby $60,538.17 will be available to pay private contractors*
> *to clear outfall ditches over the next year. Staff will be working*
> *with VDOT to determine the priority ditches as well as to seek*
> *contractors under VDOT's procurement policies. In addition, the*
> *county has been successful in receiving an additional $22,348.00*
> *in state funds for this purpose, which must be matched with local*
> *funds. The total of state and local funds available for this purpose*
> *will now be $105,234.17.*

This statement neglected mentioning that $60,538 had been allocated and was waiting to be used since the late 1990s, and half of the amount had been provided by the County in the 1993 and 1997 revenue sharing projects.

End of Year Fourteen and Fifteen:

1993-94, 1996-97, 2006-07 Revenue Sharing Projects
June 30, 2007 through June 30, 2008

Starting Balance	$60,538.17
Added	$22,348 from State
	$22,348 from County
Subtotal	$105,234.17
Amount Spent	Unknown
Balance	Unknown

September 23, 2008. Joyce McGowan, VDOT Assistant Resident Engineer (Saluda).

17 ditch-cleaning routes were completed under the revenue sharing program which has now depleted those funds.

Mr. Ingram asked how much money was in that revenue sharing fund and Mr. Whiteway responded that there was approximately $90,000.00 in the beginning of the program about four (4) to five (5) years ago.

The Commonwealth Transportation Board took action to prevent extended reallocations without activity over long spans of years, and in 2008, changes were made to section 33.1-23.05 of the Code of Virginia to deallocate projects without activity after 24 months. After years of inaction, all the funds mentioned by Administrator Whiteway in 2006 were used by September 2008.

Three Months into Year Sixteen: 1993-94, 1996-97, 2006-07
Revenue Sharing Projects, September 23, 2008
Amount Spent $60,538.17
Balance   Zero.

Early in 2014, Melinda Moran, Mathews County Administrator, could not supply any additional records on how the funds were used in 2006 – 2008 because VDOT had handled all expenses.

I contacted retired Administrator Steve Whiteway about your inquiry as he was the one who would have managed these projects at that time. It is my understanding that all expenses were handled by VDOT. I would recommend you contact them directly for details on each of these projects.

1993-4 and 1996-7 Revenue Sharing Financial Records Purged. No Info on 2006-7

Subsequently, VDOT staff advised Delegate Keith Hodges that financial statements for expenses for the 1993-94 and 1996-97 Revenue Sharing Projects had been purged, and no reports are available. VDOT offered no information on the 2006-07 Revenue Sharing Project.

Who Oversees Revenue-Sharing Projects and Finances?

VDOT approves, manages and monitors revenue-sharing projects. The Revenue Sharing Guidelines do not detail any oversight or project review after completion. It would seem that the system expects VDOT to do the right thing in carrying out the intent of the projects, but that was not the case for Mathews County's projects.

In spite of the history with the three projects in 1993, 1996 and 2006, Mathews County once again entered into a new project with VDOT in April 2013.

VDOT Offers New Revenue Sharing Outfall Study

AT A RECONVENED MEETING OF THE BOARD OF SUPERVISORS OF MATHEWS COUNTY, VIRGINIA, HELD IN THE HISTORIC COURTROOM OF THE MATHEWS COUNTY COURTHOUSE THEREOF ON TUESDAY, APRIL 23, 2013 AT 1:00 P.M. (Reconvened from April 18, 2013 Budget Public Hearing Meeting)

Mr. Trapani then recommended the Board add a cost center back to the plan that used to be utilized to address outfall ditches. He recommended they transfer approximately $15,000 to this cost center and form a partnership to develop a drainage study of *the entire County, one section at a time, and to also develop a recommended plan of action. He reviewed the proposed process with the Board. A copy of his notes are attached to these minutes.*

Utilizing the map he handed out to the Board, he recommended the initial study area consist of everything south of Rt. 608, Port Haywood. Mr. Ingram stated that the study is a great idea.

Ms. Putt questioned how much time the process would take with regard to the initial proposed study area. Mr. Trapani stated that it would be hard to tell until an actual study area has been determined. He stated that he hoped to complete the study on the proposed area and any required work within a year's time.

This time the Mathews County Board of Supervisors voted to approve $15,000 from the Six Year Secondary Improvement Plan at the request of Sean Trapani, VDOT Resident Engineer, to go toward the cost of a new outfall drainage study, starting with the area south of Route 608.

2014 Revenue Sharing Changes Gears Before It Begins

On May 28, 2013, the Board passed the formal resolution adding a study to restore drainage outfalls to the Six-Year Plan and Budget for Secondary Roads, 2014-2019. On June 25, Sean Trapani advised the Board that the money for the drainage study would be available after July 1, and he would meet with Ms. Moran to begin the process. But the project changed direction with no public discussion at either the July or August meetings of the Board of Supervisors.

8

The Shift from Outfall Drainage to Roadside BMPs

BMPs. Best Management Practices. Logic would consider it a BMP for a highway drainage system to convey rainwater from roadside ditches to functioning outfall ditches to appropriate receiving waters while still oxygenated to support the health of those waters and protect the land.

When County Administrator Mindy Moran wrote to the National Fish and Wildlife Foundation on July 29, 2013, her letter mirrored two nearly identical ones from VDOT and MPPDC in support of the MPPDC grant application for a "Rural Ditch Enhancement Study."

> *This project will provide Mathews County an opportunity to begin addressing stormwater issues associated with existing ditches both on public and private properties within the county.*

> *If funded, this proposed ditching project in Mathews County*
> *will supplement and expand a ditching project being conducted*
> *by Virginia Department of Transportation (VDOT). Through*
> *coordinated efforts between Mathews County, Draper Aden*
> *Associates, VDOT, and the MPPDC, potential causes and*
> *remedies to improve existing drainage issues and water quality*
> *within Mathews County will be identified.*

All three letters mentioned the outcome would include: "strategic analysis of existing deficiencies within the ditch system" and "preliminary analysis to determine the estimated pollutant loading reductions to be achieved with selected ditch improvements BMPs."

At this point, the proposed National Fish and Wildlife Foundation Study departed from the concept of a study to restore drainage outfalls that the Mathews County Board resolved to fund with $15,000 from the Secondary Six Year Plan in May 2013. The Board was not advised at the August meeting of the addition of BMPs, and in his statement at the September 26 Board meeting, Sean Trapani didn't mention BMPs. There was no explanation in the grant application of what water quality improvement was desired, what pollutants the "selected ditch improvement BMPs" would involve or how they had been or would be identified.

When Will They Ever Learn? 2014 Revenue Sharing Drainage Study

Oct. 22, 2013 Board of Supervisors Minutes

> *Mr. Trapani gave an update on the drainage study. He stated that*
> *he and Ms. Moran met with the Planning District commission*
> *and the engineers they have on call. He stated they were able to*
> *submit a grant application to the U.S. Fish and Wildlife* to cover*

engineering services for the drainage study with the idea that the funds from the Secondary Six-Year Program would be used for the actual work. ...He stated that he and Ms. Moran had also met with Ms. Casey and Mr. Ingram to discuss target areas.

Mr. Trapani stated that the Revenue Sharing Program is another option for funding.

These additional funds could be used for the drainage study.

December 17, 2013 Board of Supervisors Minutes

Mr. Trapani informed the Board that the Middle Peninsula Planning District Commission had been awarded a grant in the amount of $38,500 from the U. S. Fish & Wildlife Service* and that these funds, along with funds outlined in the budget for the Secondary Six-Year Plan, would be used toward drainage efforts. He stated that these funds will also be used in conjunction with Revenue Sharing funds, but that amount is unknown until the General Assembly determines the budget.

Mr. Trapani stated that his office is currently working with the Middle Peninsula Planning District Commission on a Hazard Mitigation grant that he hoped will be utilized in the drainage improvement effort.

*Note: The grant application was to the National Fish and Wildlife Foundation, a not-for-profit conservation group, not the US Fish and Wildlife Service, a federal agency. The grant was awarded to Draper Aden Associates, an engineering firm working with MPPDC.

Confirmation Outfall Restoration Replaced by BMP Construction in Right-of-Way

The Ditches of Mathews County Project asked MPPDC for a description of the scope of the NFWF grant application in April. MPPDC's response was the first public confirmation that the outfall drainage study authorized by the Mathews Board of Supervisors a year earlier had been changed from a county-wide outfall drainage restoration study in Mathews to one that would help VDOT decide how to use its "limited funding for construction of ditch improvement projects within public rights-of-way; VDOT will use this study to determine the best use of the available funding for implementation.... The results of the study will be transferrable to other counties within the region."

In practical terms, outfall drainage ditches were eliminated because they are not in the public right-of-way, leaving only roadside ditches to be studied. But it goes further than that—the engineering services were to design stormwater quality improvement BMPs. That sounds like a reasonable goal, except for the fact there is no money in the grant budget for testing of water in ditches to identify what, if any, pollutants there are to be improved, and the funds include grading and landscaping which is not possible, and not necessary, on most of the secondary roads adjacent to the ditches in Mathews.

It isn't much of a leap from grading, landscaping and stormwater quality improvement to the rain gardens and bioretention facilities BMPs Draper Aden has also utilized in other projects. One problem is urban BMPs are inappropriate for Mathews, and the other is our stormwater must be allowed to flow to receiving waters if we are ever to improve the water quality of our rivers and bays. There is no need to improve water quality in the ditches if the roadside and outfall ditches are clean and conveying fresh stormwater to receiving waters within two to three days.

9

VDOT's Lost History

Before further considering the specifics of the NFWF grant and their implications, it's important to consider VDOT's lost history. According to VDOT staff in Saluda, many old road plans have been lost or damaged, and some plans have been discarded for lack of storage space. However, numerous deeds for drainage easements and for land transfers to the Virginia Department of Transportation do exist. The information on the lost plans is duplicated in the deeds, but VDOT, as an institution, has lost track of what deeds it holds and even the location of some of the property given to the Commonwealth of Virginia for drainage by those deeds.

In 2000, a change in accounting standards by the Governmental Accounting Standards Bureau (GASB) affected Virginia's Comprehensive Annual Financial Report, and the Commonwealth had to report the value of the land under the VDOT right of way and roads and associated structures, including ditches and pipes, as assets. The value was estimated because there were no available inventories of those assets, and the Commonwealth decided the cost to retrieve the records would not have been "cost-beneficial."

INFRASTRUCTURE OWNERSHIP

VDOT has determined that the Commonwealth will capitalize the primary road system, the secondary road system, the interstate road system, state maintained bridges (including culverts) and tunnels, and the value of the land under these systems (Right of Way). VDOT has jurisdiction, control and clear ownership over the primary and interstate road systems (Right of Way). While VDOT has the jurisdiction and control over the secondary road system, ownership is not clear in many cases. However, the Commonwealth will capitalize the secondary road system since VDOT has primary responsibility for the maintenance of these systems. VDOT based its determination of ownership on guidance from GASB. The GASB 34 Implementation Guide (p. 67 Q 286) states: "When ownership is unclear, the government with primary responsibility for managing an infrastructure asset should report the asset."

All of the Right of Way in the Commonwealth is recorded, so although VDOT can obtain actual figures, the cost and time involved to obtain the right of way widths for each road would not be cost-beneficial. Each road is unique, and right of way widths are based on the needs of that particular road. (Review of the Virginia Department of Transportation's GASB 34 Infrastructure Valuation, Virginia Auditor of Public Accounts, 2000.)

VDOT Has No Permanent System for Tracking Deeds and Easements

Easements are non-depreciable assets; the value of the secondary road system is carried forward as an asset, and new acquisitions are added as assets. But it seems once the value of these assets is recorded, no one has considered requiring the Department of Transportation to be able to locate and retrieve deeds for the purchase or donation of VDOT rights-of-way or drainage easements, or the information in them, to facilitate required maintenance.

VDOT Myth: The County Clerk Holds Original Deeds to VDOT at the Courthouse.

No one in VDOT offices in Saluda, Fredericksburg or Richmond seems to be aware that original deeds have always been mailed to the Department of Transportation or the earlier Department of Highways. When the Ditches of Mathews County project asked for the location of original deeds for drainage easements or right-of-way, in order to search for Mathews drainage easements, each VDOT office consistently referred requests back to the County Courthouse, insisting the County Clerk had all the original deeds. If it weren't documented by email correspondence, it would be hard to accept the fact that a VDOT Freedom of Information Act Coordinator, Resident Engineer, Assistant Resident Engineer and a Fredericksburg District public affairs person, all believe original deeds to VDOT are kept in the County Courthouse.

Questions to VDOT under FOIA and the emailed response:

1. How are gifts, purchases and acquisitions of land from Mathews County for necessary drainage recorded by VDOT?

The Virginia Department of Transportation uses the official record of deeds at the Mathews County Courthouse to track gifts, purchases and acquisitions of land from Mathews County.

1a. Are separate records kept for Mathews County drainage through land purchased or taken by VDOT?

The Virginia Department of Transportation maintains a route file of information for individual roadways, including roadways in Mathews County. These individual files may or may not contain information on drainage as part of the maintenance records for the roadway.

2. Where are the original deeds for Mathews County with drawings of acquired land kept?

The original deeds are located at the Mathews County Courthouse.

2a. Are these original documents available for inspection?

The clerk's office for Mathews County Courthouse may have more information on the availability of the documents, as the custodian of these deeds.

Truth: Original Easement and Right-of-way Deeds Are Mailed to VDOT

When asked about the VDOT assertion that original deeds are

kept at the Courthouse, Angela Ingram, Mathews County Clerk of the Circuit Court, was surprised. She explained that after being recorded, original deeds are mailed to the location requested by the Virginia Department of Transportation. Ms. Ingram pointed out the stamp on every recorded deed page that shows to whom, where and when the deed was mailed from the County Clerk's office. She immediately contacted E. Eugene Callis, III, who held the position for 41 years before her, and he also confirmed no original deeds were ever kept at the Courthouse after being recorded. Every page in the deed books from his administration recording a deed for VDOT also has a notation to whom, where and when the actual deed was mailed.

Untracked Records Add up to Unnecessary Expense or Denial of Responsibility

VDOT's near-total lack of knowledge of their deeded outfall drainage easements and a complete denial of responsibility for their maintenance has contributed to flooded roadside ditches, woods and property. The lack of a coherent system to track drainage easements results in unnecessary expense every time there is more than minimal work on the roads or drainage systems because a VDOT staff person must physically visit the County Courthouse and go through the State Highway Plat Books or Deed Grantor/Grantee Books to look for information.

Finding drainage easement information is not straightforward. The State Highway Plat Books were established in 1950. There are no copies of VDOT's road plan sheets prior to 1950 in the books showing right-of-way or easements unless a project was still in process at that time. Hard-surfacing of primary and secondary roads began in Mathews County in 1926, and the Virginia Department of Highways built some of those roads between

1906 and 1925—which means there is no easy way of tracing right-of-way and easement deeds created before 1950.

Going through the grantor/grantee books is a time-consuming and labor-intensive process and not always successful because some of the early land donations were made as part of a petition for a public road to the County, who in turn, petitioned the Department of Highways through a Board of Supervisors resolution.

Plan sheets in the State Highway Plat Books show the names of property owners at the time of the plan and do not record all of the names in which deeds were granted to VDOT. For example, several children inherit a share in a family home. They would each sign the deed, but it would only be listed under the first person's or couple's name in the Courthouse deed Grantor Books and under the name of the deceased owner's estate on the plan sheet.

Even for those plans drawn after 1950, there is no index to the four State Highway Plat Books in Mathews County. The plan sheets are not kept together by route or project. Later revisions may have different project numbers, and there is no listing of earlier plans by project number, and no copies of plans at all for revisions without new rights-of-way or easements. Each individual plan sheet shows an easement or right-of-way from one property owner, and the sheet is added to the latest State Highway Plat Book after the County Clerk records the deed.

In addition to these difficulties, VDOT staff members with a high degree of responsibility for maintenance oversight are unaware of the number of drainage easements in Mathews County, so it's questionable how much effort is expended on Courthouse record searches.

Impact of Lost VDOT History

> *Code of Virginia § 33.1-223.2:4. Department to maintain*
> *drainage easements*

> *Whenever, in connection with or as a precondition to the*
> *construction or reconstruction of any highway, the Department*
> *shall have acquired any permanent drainage easement, the*
> *Department shall, until such time as such easement shall have*
> *been terminated, perform repairs required to protect the roadway*
> *and to ensure the proper function of the easement within the*
> *right-of-way and within the boundaries of such easement.*

When considering maintenance requirements of VDOT's roadside and outfall drainage systems, the statements, "...to ensure the proper function of the easement" and "within the boundaries of such easement" seem to be specific enough not to cause any confusion. Yet that has not been the case.

> *It's not VDOT's responsibility to clean outfall ditches unless there's*
> *a deeded easement, and there are only 14 in the county that are*
> *deeded to the Commonwealth. (Joyce McGowan, VDOT Saluda*
> *Assistant Residency Administrator, Mathews County Board of*
> *Supervisors Meeting, January 2013.)*

This chapter identifies 15 drainage easements: 14 in less than 3 miles of state roads, 11 on one road and 3 more on two specific related properties, plus one in another part of the County. The 2012 VDOT Mileage Tables show 138 miles of secondary and 32 miles of primary roads in Mathews County, and there are many times more than 15 deeded outfall and drainage easements in Mathews County along those roads.

Does anyone in VDOT remember this 1938 deeded agreement? It is unusual, and fortunate for us, because the sketch of buildings on the property, the ditch and other features are on the back of the deed itself, instead of being part of a road plan or in a County plat book.

The landowner grants to the Commonwealth, its successors and assigns, the perpetual right to maintain existing drainage ditch for the purpose of draining a road in the State Highway System now designated as Route No. 14, upon and across the lands and property of the landowner adjacent to said road, and including the right of egress and ingress to same. The center of said drainage ditch follows or is to follow the course located and marked on the sketch found on the reverse side of this sheet.

IT IS AGREED between the parties hereto that the Commonwealth shall have the right to inspect the said drainage ditch and to cut and clear all undergrowth and other obstructions in and along the said drainage ditch or adjacent thereto that may in any way endanger or interfere with the proper use of the same.

Capt. J. A. Armistead
January 12, 1938

The deed was recorded in Deed Book 34, page 395, and has a notation, "Mailed to the Department of Highways, 3/17/38."

When landowners donated their land for roads and drainage or accepted a token payment of one dollar, they trusted that the Department of Highways, and later, the Department of Transportation, would maintain the roads, including the drainage system as agreed. Otherwise, there is no reason they would sign deeds to the Commonwealth with statements like this:

...together with the right and easement to use such additional areas as may be necessary for the proper construction and maintenance of ditch easement as shown on plans.

But VDOT hasn't kept their side of the agreements. They haven't tracked the plan notations, nor the deeds, nor the locations. And even when road plans are in the State Highway Plat Books and the deeds easily identified, VDOT still has not maintained the outfalls. A clear example is Route 611 in Mathews.

There are at least 6 recorded outfall easements in the mile and a half along Route 611 (Church Street) between Route 14 (John Clayton Memorial Highway) to the north and Route 621 (Glebe Road) to the southeast.

Projects 0611-057-102 and 0611-057-104

Outlet Ditch Length	Name on Plan
1075' (cleanout)	Thomas J. Hunley
1075' (cleanout)	Cecil M. Sibley
575'	Granville Hughes
277'	Williams Pembleton
376'	John Gwynn
377'	Joseph Hall

There may be other ditch easements on the north side of Route 611 from the original plans that have not yet been identified, because this was one of the early roads in the County connecting Route 14 to the old Courthouse village.

Another extensive network of VDOT outfall and storage ditches with deeded drainage easements lies just past the intersection of Main Street and Route 611 (Tabernacle Road). These ditches ran from Tabernacle Road parallel to Main Street and around the perimeter of several properties and connected to three ditches that ran perpendicular to Main Street. The network was intended to take stormwater from Main Street and hold it when the tide was high in Put In Creek.

At the next low tide, the retained water then drained back through a cross pipe under Main Street through an outfall to Put In Creek. The network also allowed some stormwater to flow down Tabernacle Road toward Garden Creek. None of these Project 0611-057-113 ditches with deeded easements have been maintained in recent decades, and the ditch to the Main Street cross pipe is filled today with full-grown trees.

A few examples of these outfall ditch easements:

Ditch Length	Name on Deed
410′	Newport News General and Non-sectarian Hospital Association
400′	Richard Stoops
675′	Richard Sadler
530′	John Smith
530′	Mattie Thomas

Another source of land and drainage easement donations was through petitions to the Board of Supervisors for the establishment of a public road. A group of landowners along the proposed new road would agree to donate all necessary land for the road and accompanying drainage. They had the proposed road surveyed, signed a petition with their consent and waiver of notice and after a board of road viewers agreed the road was necessary for public use, the landowners presented the documents to the Supervisors. If the Supervisors concurred the road was necessary for public use, they sent a resolution to the Commonwealth requesting establishment as a state road. (The record of these petitions is found in the Board of Supervisors Minutes Books. All of the landowner names are listed, but the location of the road in early requests was given by local landmarks, which may not be easily recognized today.)

Nine Months of Board Requests and VDOT's Incorrect Responses

If a full inventory of drainage easements were available to VDOT staff in 2001, the following nine-month sequence of events might have led to a resolution of the actual problem. Not only was the problem misidentified, it was made worse, and then-current Resident Engineer Marcie Parker gave the Board incorrect information, denying the existence of a VDOT drainage easement, when in fact, at least three exist. Twelve years later, the initial problem has still not been resolved; the high school field still floods, as does the homeowner's property across the road. And VDOT has not advised the Board of Supervisors of the existence of the outfall easements.

The parties involved are 2001-02 Supervisors Ingram, Sadler and Rowe. Alfred Harris, VDOT Superintendent (Mathews), Marcie Parker, VDOT Resident Engineer (Saluda) and property owners, Mr. and Mrs. Frank Davis. The locations: The Davis property on the opposite side of Route 14/198 from Mathews High School, the High School property along Route 14/198 and from 14/198 to the outfall to Stutts Creek behind the school's athletic field.

This saga begins with a Board Supervisor's request to the local VDOT superintendent.

> Mr. Ingram asked Mr. Harris to check the outfall ditch behind the high school; Mr. Harris agreed to this request. (Board of Supervisors Minutes, June 24, 2001.)

*Mr. Sadler asked Ms. Parker and Mr. Harris to study a standing
water problem on the property of Mrs. Davis, located across the
street from the high school. Ms. Parker agreed. (Mathews Board
of Supervisors Minutes, July 24, 2001.)*

*Mr. Sadler asked Ms. Parker if VDOT has had a chance to look
at Mr. Frank Davis's property and the standing water problem.
Mr. Alfred Harris of VDOT reported that they have been to Mr.
Davis's property and have cut the ditch along the roadside in the
hopes that this will correct the standing water problem. (Mathews
Board of Supervisors Minutes, September 25, 2001.)*

*Mr. Harris reported to the Board that the ditch behind the
high school has been cleaned. (Board of Supervisors Minutes,
December 18, 2001.)*

*With regard to Mr. Rowe's question about improving drainage
ditches at Mathews High School to help alleviate flooding in the
school, Ms. Parker noted that Mr. Harris has cleared enough to
prevent flooding and will complete the project as weather allows.
(Board of Supervisors Minutes, January 24, 2002.)*

*Ms. Parker informed the Board that the ditch cleaning at the high
school has been completed; however, this ditch is not a VDOT-
maintained ditch and therefore the school should be prepared
to take on the responsibility of maintaining same in the future.
(Mathews Board of Supervisors Minutes, March 26, 2002.)*

These exchanges might seem reasonable except for the 1985
VDOT plan sheet for Route 14/198 in front of the high school
and a recorded deed for a drainage easement from the County
Board of Education.

The Details

Page 211 in State Highway Plat Book 3 is from project number 0014 057 305 M501, PE-101, RW 201, Sheet 7.

Easement 1 is shown as a dot-dashed line in the lower right corner of the plan sheet indicating a prior permanent easement. This prior easement line runs from the County park diagonally toward the high school with a notation of "Athletic Field" in the center. (A notation below that is illegible, possibly a compass reading.) The easement jogs at an angle toward the outfall to Stutts Creek that runs along the high school athletic field. Although the diagram ends before the line connects, it is the most likely point of connection for the water to flow.

Easement 2. From the Davis Property. Not shown on this plan sheet is another 1973 deeded drainage outfall easement crossing Route 621, Glebe Road taken by VDOT from the Davis family (Deed Book 89, page 167). The deed book record of the certificate estimating the value of the land mentions two drainage ditches. One is the outfall that runs behind the First Baptist Church from Glebe Road to 14/198 and is supposed to drain through the cross pipe in front of the Davis property toward the high school as shown on page 211 plan sheet.

Easement 3. From the Mathews County School Board. At the end of the cross pipe from the Davis property, there is a 30" pipe which runs from the shoulder of the road across the parking area to a point alongside the athletic field. The easement is 130' x 18' to maintain this pipe.

Where it connects and the exact location of the outlet is not shown. It is on another plan sheet, indicated by the notation of: *Match Line Sta 12+00 Sheet 7*. At the northwest end of the plan sheet, there is also another notation: *Match Line Sta 61+00 Sheet No. 8*. There is no reference to the previous plan number which should have been indicated when the revised plan was created. No plan sheet has turned up in the State Highway Plat Books yet that matches—but it existed when this newer plan was drawn.

The Result of VDOT Not Having Easement Details

State Highway Plat Book page 211 plan sheet shows notations for graded roadside ditches. When Alfred Harris cut the ditch deeper, as reported in the September 2001 Board minutes, this would have interfered with the hydraulic action of the ditch and worsened the drainage function in the long run.

In October 2001, the Mathews Transportation Safety Commission made the high school outfall one of the 1A priority outfalls to be handled by the Revenue Sharing Projects.

Mr. Harris said the outfall behind the school had been cleaned in December 2001, but Ms. Parker acknowledged in January 2002, there was more to be done "when weather allowed." When she returned at the March Board meeting to say it was done, she did not refer to the revenue sharing project or indicate heavy equipment had been used.

There was at least $60,538.17 in unspent funds from the 1993-94 and 1996-97 Revenue Sharing funds that could have been used in 2002 for the necessary heavy equipment. There is no record what additional work was done in 2002, but since the problem is still occurring, it's likely the outfall was not properly or completely cleaned. There's no indication whether the pipes were cleaned. But Marci Parker in 2002 laid the burden of future maintenance on the County when VDOT did indeed hold drainage easements for the location and is responsible.

A discussion with VDOT officials in Saluda in August 2013 revealed they were unaware of the existence of these easements, which raises more questions. Did VDOT fail to do the research at the Courthouse to look for an easement under Ms. Parker's administration, or did the person looking miss it? Either way, the Board of Supervisors was given wrong information, and the high school has suffered through another 12 years of flooding on their property.

Outfalls Are Essential to Drainage—How Many Deeds Does VDOT Need to Prove It

Roadside ditches connecting to channelized streams and outfall ditches that lead to receiving waters form an intricate network that emulates the watershed's drainage pattern before there were roads. This is the pre-development hydrology that all stormwater goals seek to replicate.

How many deeds would it take for VDOT to recognize they do have a responsibility to convey stormwater from the roads to a receiving body of water without causing harm to property, woods, streams or the Bay—or the roads themselves?

Where Did the Outfall Inventory Go?

Joyce McGowan, the Assistant Resident Engineer at Saluda said in a discussion after the August 2012 board meeting that she and Resident Engineer Don Wagner personally walked and inventoried all of the outfall ditches in Mathews county in connection with the 1993 Mathews County revenue-sharing project. When a request was made for a copy of the 1993 Outfall Inventory, VDOT could not locate it in Saluda, Mathews, Fredericksburg or Richmond.

Re: Stormwater Outfall Inventory

Thank you for your inquiry. VDOT is currently developing outfall inventories in those urbanized areas regulated under our MS4 permit. Since Matthews County is not currently a part of our MS4 regulated area, we have no current plans to perform outfall inventories within that area. If you need information about an outfall in a specific area of Matthews County, you might contact the VDOT Saluda Residency Office.

(Email, Roy Mills, VDOT StormWaterWeb, January 31, 2012)

I have not been able to locate any of the files that I had on this from the earlier years. I have looked in the attic and in the files, but I can't locate any of them. ...

Sorry I couldn't be of further assistance. (Email, Saluda Assistant Resident Engineer, September 11, 2012.)

Thank you for contacting The Department of Transportation with your question. Unfortunately, we do not have a copy of this document at the District. If the Saluda Residency cannot locate this, I am not sure what assistance can be further provided. I suggest contacting the Saluda Residency again and seeing if Joyce can possibly research this further.

Best regards (Email, Fredericksburg District, October 16, 2012)

Neither the Mathews County administrator nor the Planning and Zoning Office has a copy of the outfall ditch inventory. While there are references to "attached" material in Board Minutes, any attachments related to outfall ditches were not retained according to Mathews County Administrator Melinda Moran in August 2013.

VDOT Only Tracks Easement Information for Current Projects

VDOT's Right of Way and Utility Management 1999 software has full right of way and easement information—and can't track it after the conclusion of the project.

> *Implemented in early September of 1999, the client-server Right of Way and Utilities Management System RUMS solution has not only met, but exceeded the Division's desires. RUMS provides management with up to the minute highway project statuses through ad hoc queries as well as reports served over a secure Intranet... Division agents have found their workload reduced as data entered into RUMS is now able to feed to a myriad of letters and other documents - letters and documents which RUMS stores in a centralized Oracle database. (VDOT, http://www. virginiadot.org/business/row-rums.asp)*

> *iRUMS is not available for viewing by the public, because it serves as a storehouse of information on citizens and the location and value of their land parcels. Legal information available on iRUMS includes title orders, deeds, condemnations, condemnation orders, multiple owners on a property (if applicable), relocations, appeals, and payments made for a property. (Sande Snead, Public Roads, 2005.)*

It seems VDOT is protecting public information from public access. Perhaps those responsible for iRUMS are unaware the information they're protecting is available to the public through county websites and courthouses. VDOT deeds, payments, court orders, condemnation orders, property owners and land value are all available in County Courthouse public records. If any other sensitive information in the files needs to be protected, it could be coded in such a way to require password access.

The Public Can't Use iRums—VDOT Staff Can't Either

Your interest in our Right of Way & Utilities Management
System (RUMS) is appreciated. As you noted, RUMS is primarily
a tracking system for our right of way acquisition process and
property management activities. While we can use RUMS
to retrieve information about some past acquisitions, the
local courthouses are still the best source to find out detailed
information about property transfers to VDOT. RUMS also does
not cross-reference projects. (Email correspondence from VDOT
Right of Way & Utilities Division, Aug. 1, 2013.)

This statement means there is still no way for VDOT to easily identify right-of-way and easements without time-consuming searches of courthouse records. When future work is needed on roads or drainage systems VDOT should be maintaining, there's no straightforward way to access information VDOT has or had in its computers.

The absence of a system to track deeded property, especially pre-1950 transactions, along with the fact that the Saluda Residency and Fredericksburg District do not have an inventory of the outfall ditches in Mathews County, results in an entity responsible for moving stormwater off roads through channels it will not maintain and may not be able to locate.

10

Ditch Problems 101

Most causes of highway drainage failures are obvious once they are identified. When ditches are flooded though, the problems are hidden under water or debris, and attempts to make corrections can make matters worse. Another reason ditch work should not be done in the winter rainy season.

When Ditches of Mathews County volunteers investigated VDOT drainage failures, the same issues surfaced time and again--improper slope or depth, blockages, improper or neglected maintenance. Other problems and VDOT practices play a part as well.

The following list highlights the most frequently encountered problems, with notes on related issues. (See Appendix A for basic information on ditch components and function.)

Observed Causes of Ditch Failure

Improper Ditch Slope

Ditches depend on slope to maintain hydraulic flow. Slope errors exist in ditches throughout the County. VDOT does not use transits or laser levels to assure proper slope when using an excavator for cleaning ditches or installing pipes. Excavation while ditches are flooded prevents identification of slope errors.

Incorrect Ditch Depth

Ditch channels must be in proper alignment with pipes to maintain flow and empty properly. This is not the case in many ditches in Mathews.

Blocked Flow - Pipe Failure

There is no single estimate for the service life of corrugated metal pipes because pH and flow rate of water passing through them, as well as the moisture level and pH of the surrounding soil, affect their durability. In general though, corrugated metal pipe has a service life of 50 to 100 years with higher moisture and lower pH reducing service life. Many of the pipes installed in the 1930s and 1940s are approaching or have reached the end of their serviceable life.

There is no county-wide inventory of pipes or schedule for replacement. Annual or biennial inspections of roadways do not include pipes, only features visible to the driver from within the inspection van or to the cameras underneath.

Based on the number of pipes that had to be located by use of maps, then probing and clearing of weeds and mud over and around them during the course of research for this book, it appears cleaning is done or replacements are made only when citizens report and complain long enough about a pipe failure or when the failure causes flooding across a road surface. Pipe cleaning should be done on a watershed basis to maintain drainage; even one blocked pipe at a critical location can back up stormwater for a large area.

When cement pipes separate or crack and leak while in service, the roadway is undermined. When washouts form as a result, the pipes are not automatically replaced, but patched with asphalt instead. In some cases, pipes have been filled in with patching material permanently blocking the flow of water they were intended to convey. In other cases, the patches fall into the pipe, holes open again and new patches are eventually applied.

Blocked Flow - Sediment in Pipes

VDOT sold its pipe cleaning trucks as a cost-saving measure. Because rentals run in the neighborhood of $20,000 a week, VDOT uses them on a limited basis. With no county-wide inventory, there is no organized preventive maintenance program. Pipes not cleaned on a regular basis for decades allow sediment to develop into full blockages. Failure to clean and maintain culverts and pipes under roads blocks stream flow and causes an accumulation of water on the uphill side and inadequate flow to maintain the channel on the downhill side. If blockages aren't cleared, all water up-slope of the blockage is impacted.

Blocked Flow - Debris From VDOT Actions

Gravel roads are scraped to remove pine straw and then new gravel is laid down instead of using power rake equipment designed for straw removal that would leave the gravel in place. Gravel, pine straw and leaf litter are pushed into ditches in the process. Some of the debris moves into pipes, further blocking them. Rotoditching or excavating used to remove the piles of debris in the ditches cuts into the shoulders and destroys some, leaving no margin between the ditches and the roadbed and breaking off the ends of concrete pipes under the roads. In 2014, snowplows pushed dirt and debris into ditches, and cleanup after the snow plow broke off and pushed sections of the shoulders into the ditches as well.

Channelized Streams

VDOT stream channelization for road building, widening and realignment in the 1920s through 1980s may not be up to current standards. Some pipes are too small; some blocked; none are maintained regularly.

Obstructions to flow caused by blocked pipes, VDOT rotoditching or excavation force flow overland flow through woods damaging timber crops and risk *E. coli* transfer to TMDL waters.

Mowing Practices

Mowing is done on a hit-or-miss basis, and it is often delayed until invasive growth is 2 to 4 ft high or more. Muck forms from cuttings dropped into the ditches after the dissolved oxygen in the standing water is exhausted. Because of the degree of overgrowth, the operator cannot see the ends of pipes which go under the road; the mower runs over pipes, breaking off the ends. This causes more blockages in the pipes and cracks that can lead to complete pipe failure. VDOT says tree seedlings don't interfere with drainage while small and doesn't mow or cut them. When larger, they block drainage, but VDOT doesn't cut them because they claim they are unable to deal with larger trees.

Cyanobacteria

Cyanobacteria (also known as blue-green algae) form dense mats that can block drainage flow and deoxygenate water preventing decomposition of leaf litter and leading to further blockage.

Cyanobacteria also produce toxins and nitrous oxide, a greenhouse gas.

Outfalls

VDOT's progressive reduction of maintenance for budget reasons over the past 40 years allows full-grown and/or fallen trees and overgrown vegetation to interrupt flow to receiving waters.

Blocked pipes under roads from roadside ditches prevent flow to outfalls.

There is no system to locate VDOT deeds or records of them, to identify where outfalls were required by road plans, especially for those prior to 1950. Early road plans are often no longer available.

Erosion Caused by VDOT Practices

VDOT's current practices are causing more erosion than previously existed. The shoulder at Ward's Corner at Routes 198 and 14 is eroding into the outfall, uncovering the pipe and causing a safety issue on the shoulder; two adjacent bank failures were covered by riprap without clearing the ditch obstructions.

VDOT ditch excavation and rotoditching does not preserve proper ditch bank angles and results in vertical sides that are prone to slope failure with a portion of the wall sliding into the ditch to obstruct the flow. The slope failures on Route 198 (Buckley Hall Road) from Hudgins to Cobbs Creek are an example of this problem, but it is present in many ditch banks on secondary roads as well.

Clean Water Act, TMDLs and Mathews County

Virginia must set water quality standards for all waterbodies to meet the requirements of the Clean Water Act. Our local waters have two levels of standards for *E. coli* bacteria: one for recreational uses of swimming and fishing and a much stricter one for safe harvesting of shellfish for human consumption.

TMDL means Total Maximum Daily Load and represents the amount of a pollutant that a body of water can handle without violating the standards for that material. The only TMDL pollutant in Mathews County so far is *E. coli*, a fecal coliform bacteria. A water quality improvement plan was approved by the Commonwealth in 2013, and by the EPA on August 28, 2014 for some Mathews creeks in the Piankatank, Milford Haven, Gwynn's Island watershed to reduce the levels of *E. coli*. The plan included septic tank pump outs and repairs, use of agricultural buffers near waterways and reduction of dog and wildlife waste reaching the waters. The plan also recommended the establishment of a Ditch Maintenance Task Force. Although VDOT District Administrator Quintin Elliott agreed to participate in such a task force, the Commonwealth took no action to convene one.

A Water Quality Improvement Plan, also called a TMDL Implementation Plan (IP), is written for a specific watershed or an important part of one. Knowing where the water flows and what areas are impaired suggests where it might be picking up pollution. The Virginia DEQ (Department of Environmental Quality) improved their original GIS computer maps to come closer to actual conditions and watershed boundaries. With the help of citizen representatives on the TMDL Steering Committee, DEQ also corrected the statistics on numbers of people, dogs, livestock and wildlife and adjusted the number of septic system failures to reflect actual conditions. But the DEQ maps given to the TMDL workgroups had no land use code for rural residential areas, so all occupied areas were shown as urban. At 104 people per square mile, the population density of Mathews is far less than Williamsburg's 1,532 or Richmond's 3,269 persons per square mile.

The latest 2012 agricultural census shows cattle numbers in the county declined to 122 from 1,352 in 1925 (the earliest year with livestock details). In 2012, there were 4,646 acres of farmland, down from 43,205 acres in 1910. Most farmers in Mathews use continuous no-till operations with controlled application of liquid fertilizer instead of the former use of manure to reduce the amount of sediment and excess nutrients reaching our waters. They are aware of and use vegetative buffers near water, so agriculture in Mathews is not a significant source of *E. coli*.

In every TMDL creek area, VDOT ditches are impacted by neglected maintenance and do not allow a free flow of rainwater to the TMDL waters. Department of Health shoreline sanitation surveys noted flooded VDOT ditches in areas where condemnations were later posted. Saturated soil reduces the efficiency of septic systems, whether this was a factor, or the interruption of the flow of oxygenated rainwater encourages the growth of naturalized *E. coli* remains to be seen. When ditches don't convey stormwater, flooding into wooded areas adds the risk of picking up wildlife waste and carrying it to TMDL waters.

E. coli is the only pollutant, but *E. coli* contamination is not the only impairment in our waters. The other major impairment is low levels of dissolved oxygen. Without oxygen in the water, beneficial bacteria cannot decompose plant matter. This leads to an accumulation of mucky sediments that provides a food source and shelters *E. coli* in the water from sun. Natural predators of *E. coli* need oxygen, but *E. coli* can survive without it and can live for months outside of a human or animal host. (Kashian, 2010.)

Low dissolved oxygen levels are an impairment, not a specific pollutant, and in Mathews, not directly caused by excessive nutrients, and so it was not included in the TMDL Plan. There is also no easy way to restore oxygen levels. A first step, though, is the commonsense approach of letting rainwater with its natural supply of oxygen reach our waterways instead of being held in stagnant flooded ditches until all the oxygen is used up.

By restoring the flow from roadside and outfall ditches, cyanobacteria will no longer be able to colonize the ditches and add to water quality issues by using up oxygen, releasing toxins and greenhouse gases and impairing the clarity of our waters. The increase in oxygenated water will allow beneficial bacteria to decompose plant matter completely leading to clearer waters and permit microbial predators to feed on *E. coli*. More oxygenated water will support all aquatic life, including subaqueous vegetation which requires dissolved oxygen in the water at night and on cloudy days.

The 2014 National Fish and Wildlife Foundation study may help move toward establishing the Ditch Maintenance Task Force recommended in the Piankatank, Milford Haven, Gwynn's Island TMDL Implementation Plan to work on ways to resolve the issue of blocked and flooded ditches to allow fresh rainwater to reach the TMDL streams.

11

VDOT Myths and Road Damage

VDOT Myth: Stormwater standing in the ditches has no impact on roadbed integrity. (Fredericksburg District Administrator, Quintin D. Elliott, March 2013)

VDOT HAS IGNORED THEIR OFFICIAL Drainage Manual and Best Practices Manual for over twenty years. "The Department assumes full maintenance responsibility within the limits of the drainage easement." (VDOT Maintenance Best Practices, p 69, July 30, 2010.) Although this seems to be a clear-cut and reasonable statement, VDOT officials in Fredericksburg and Saluda reject it.

Many of the current problems with the road drainage system in Mathews County evolved with the Virginia Department of Transportation mythology of why VDOT is not responsible for the ditches. But budget cuts that failed to recognize the connection of proper stormwater conveyance to the health of our rivers and bays added to the effects of neglected maintenance.

VDOT's Biennial Report on the Condition of and Investment Needed to Maintain and Operate the Existing Surface Transportation Infrastructure for FY 2011 and FY 2012 points out the failure to distinguish between urban landscape amenities and essential rural drainage.

> ...some services such as vegetation management or drainage management are considered less important than investment related activities on pavements and bridges.

This attitude could be the reason VDOT doesn't connect lack of adequate vegetation control in ditches and inadequate drainage system maintenance with premature roadway failure. Yes, there are other reasons for pavement damage. The question then is why three road segments have the same road damage when they have a wide range of Average Annual Daily Traffic (2011)?

Route 611—Church Street from Route 14 to Main Street
2100 trips

Route 608—Hamburg Road from Route 14 to Route 609—
Bethel Beach Road
560 trips

Route 677—Canoe Yard Trail from Route 611 to Route 609
90 trips

Maybe it is a coincidence all three have flooded ditches along much of their length and that horizontal movement of the water from the ditches can lead to saturated roadbeds. But according to Federal Highway Administration information, it's no coincidence.

...if the pavement system is saturated only 10% of its life (e.g., about one month per year), a pavement section with a moderate stability factor will be serviceable only about 50% of its fully drained performance period....it is practically impossible to completely seal the pavement, especially from moisture that may enter from the sides or beneath the pavement section.

(Federal Highway Administration (FHWA), Geotechnical Aspects of Pavements Reference Manual.)

Considering these statements, why does VDOT permit stormwater to remain for months in blocked roadside ditches where it can move through the sides of the roadbed or below the pavement, particularly when the roadbed has been elevated? Unfortunately, the extreme cold episodes in January 2014 resulted in severe freezing heave damage as predicted in the FHWA Pavements Reference Manual.

The damaging effects of excess moisture on the pavement have long been recognized. Moisture from a variety of sources can enter a pavement structure. This moisture, in combination with heavy traffic loads and freezing temperatures, can have a profound negative effect on both material properties and the overall performance of a pavement system.

Excessive moisture within a pavement structure can adversely affect pavement performance. A pavement can be stable at a given moisture content, but may become unstable if the materials become saturated.... Subsurface water can freeze, expand, and exert forces of considerable magnitude on a given pavement.

When Reports Don't Match Reality — Ditches Fail and Roads Suffer

VDOT's Biennial Needs report says VDOT uses the frequency of work required to maintain ditches able to handle 50-year storm events to determine their needs for drainage management. Yet highway ditches throughout Mathews County are unable to handle even a minor storm event, and VDOT officials still insist they have no responsibility unless water is over the traffic lanes. Remember Quintin Elliott's statement: "Stormwater standing in the ditches has no impact on roadbed integrity."

Why then does VDOT tell the governor, the Joint Legislative Audit and Review Commission and the Commonwealth Transportation Board a different story in the Fiscal Year 2011/12 Biennial Needs Report?

Drainage management includes all maintenance activities performed on drainage assets such as ditches, pipes, curb and gutter, slopes, rock slide protection, retaining walls, and storm water basins. These assets work as a system to move water off of and way [sic] from pavements and bridges where it can contribute to more rapid deterioration of those assets. The size, capacity and configuration of drainage assets such as pipes and ditches are specified to accommodate water equivalent to 50 year storm events. While their physical condition does not necessarily determine whether they perform adequately, it is closely associated with their performance.

Service standards for drainage focus on their performance and on the timeliness of maintenance when these assets fail.

Figure 2 of VDOT's 2013 Annual Report to the governor and the members of the General Assembly proves the accuracy of these statements, showing a steady decline in the percentage of secondary roads with a fair or better rating from 65.8% to 59.6% between 2010 and 2013. The report recognizes a greater need and lists an 18% increase for Roadside Services.

> *Funds needed to provide roadside services needs total $460 million, an increase of $69 million (18 percent) when compared to FY 2014-2015 needs. This category includes drainage management, vegetation management, and sound barrier management.*

But the 18% number masks the 28% increase for drainage needs by combining it with 3% for vegetation management and 4% for sound barriers. The explanation for the increases supports the statements made here in Chapter 9.

> *The increase in drainage and sound wall needs is the result of an update in inventory, indicating more drainage assets and sound walls on the secondary system than previously recorded. The increase in vegetation management needs is due primarily to an increase in tree removal needs where tree failure is imminent and risk of damage is high.*

We can't say with certainty how many of those trees should have been removed as seedlings with appropriate "vegetation management" and how many might be a risk because of storm damage, but the increase in recognizing drainage assets is a direct result of failing to adequately track inventory when it was acquired or constructed.

There is no justification for over 30 years of failing ditches due to lack of maintenance, denial of responsibility, inadequate recordkeeping or created myths.

12

When Drainage Studies
Don't Study Drainage

WHEN DOES A DRAINAGE STUDY measure how to pay for "ownership research, compile historical knowledge and acquiring right of entry?"

It happened when MPPDC (Middle Peninsula Planning District Commission) ignored preliminary findings by the Ditches of Mathews County Project about VDOT maintenance failures and the impact on Mathews County and continued with plans for a study to determine "ownership of the ditches." Part of this study was initially intended to support a plan to reassign responsibility for outfall ditch maintenance from the Virginia Department of Transportation to the county or to individual property owners.

The MPPDC applied for and received a 2012 Coastal Zone Management Program Grant from the Virginia Department of Environmental Quality. The grant application stated:

> *With the assistance of legal research, MPPDC staff will assess the ownership, management and oversight of stormwater ditches (perpendicular to the VDOT ROW) and the relationship to the secondary road system overseen by the Virginia Department of Transportation. Rural outfall ditches play an important role in the movement of stormwater in rural localities. If outfall ditches remain clogged and are located on private property, who has the responsibility to treat stormwater which originates from VDOT infrastructure? MPPDC staff will also explore the formation of a regional stormwater management program to reduce the cost and improve the delivery of stormwater management services. (Lewie Lawrence, MPPDC Executive Director, personal communication, 2012.)*

This study was described in the information packet for the July 2013 MPPDC meeting.

> *Corresponded with John Morris, Beale, Davidson, Etherington & Morris, P.C., concerning files documenting information on ditches in Gloucester, Mathews, and Middlesex Counties. As part of this project, Mr. Morris is conducting legal research to assess the ownership, management, and oversight of stormwater ditches that are perpendicular and parallel to the VDOT right-of-way (ROW) and the relationship to the secondary road system overseen by VDOT.*

This description added the roadside ditches, shifting the focus from outfall ditches that carry stormwater from roadside ditches to receiving bodies of water. Why the Department of Environmental Quality allowed this is a mystery, because the Commonwealth of Virginia's Comprehensive Annual Report has recorded the secondary road system overseen by VDOT, including roadside ditches, pipes and culverts, as an infrastructure asset since 2002.

Outfall ditches may be on land belonging to individuals; VDOT may or may not have an easement on the land next to outfall ditches; streams channelized by VDOT for use as outfalls may cross private or public land. In each case, the water is claimed as "state waters" by the Code of Virginia, whether it's in roadside or outfall ditches or streams.

> *"State waters" means all water, on the surface and under the ground, wholly or partially within or bordering the Commonwealth or within its jurisdiction, including wetlands. (Code of Virginia, § 62.1-44.3)*

Freshly Fallen Rain Is Not Polluted

Stormwater in Mathews County ditches has not been used for any purpose, and it has not been altered by the residents or Mathews County. It is not polluted. It contains life-supporting oxygen when fresh. If natural precipitation flows to a receiving body of water promptly after falling without alteration, stormwater has no need for treatment. This same fresh stormwater with its oxygen supply is necessary for the health of our waterways and the lifeforms that depend on them. The DEQ and DCR are concerned with stormwater runoff causing erosion or picking up urban pollution, but when discussing stormwater, they make no statements about the need for rural rainfall to follow its natural watershed drainage patterns to maintain stream vitality.

History Repeats Itself When DEQ Accepts Flawed MPPDC Grant Study Reports

The Virginia Department of Environmental Quality, Coastal Zone Management Division, and NOAA have failed in the past to ensure accuracy in grant study reports by MPPDC, and history repeated itself with the 2013 MPPDC Roadside and Outfall Drainage Ditches report.

Citizens presented statements at the MPPDC December 2013 meeting pointing out errors in the report and asked that the MPPDC vote to reject the report until it was corrected. While the commissioners acknowledged there were errors, they still voted to accept the September 3, 2013 report on Roadside and Outfall Drainage Ditches.

Examples of Flaws in MPPDC's Roadside and Outfall Drainage Ditches Report

The report did not acknowledge the Code of Virginia § 62.1-44.3 claims all surface water in streams or ditches as "state waters."

The report did not differentiate between natural streams used as outfalls by VDOT or ditches created to serve that purpose, assuming easements would be necessary for both. VDOT needs no easement from a landowner to use a stream as an outfall—unless VDOT needs access to the stream for maintenance from private property. Since pipes from one side of the road to the other are always in the right-of-way, no additional easement is needed for installation, cleaning and maintenance of roadside pipes.

Arbitrary statements, without evidence, ignored VDOT's policies of setting drainage standards and requirements for acceptance of roads into the state secondary road system.

The report based conclusions on the incorrect assumption that all secondary roads still have the same 30-ft prescriptive easements as after the Byrd Act in 1932, ignoring new rights-of-way and easements obtained when roads were widened or re-aligned by the Commonwealth.

The report incorrectly states homeowners are responsible for repair or replacement of entrance pipes. In areas with ditches in the VDOT right-of-way, the Code of Virginia 24VAC30-73-90, E2 specifically says that VDOT is responsible for the drainage pipe at the entrance on highways with ditches.

The report assumes, in more than one example, low elevation and not blocked VDOT pipes as the reason for water accumulated on one side of the road and its failure to pass to the other side, even when water at a lower elevation further along in the same channel does flow. Cameras were not used to examine the condition or degree of blockage of cross pipes, and statements were based on external observation, even where some pipes were submerged.

The report did not consider under-the-road pipe failure. It made no notation of road washouts over a pipe in one location, and in another, blamed elevation for a collapsed pipe on the outlet side of the road.

In one case, the report did not consider VDOT plan notations of "special design ditches" which are roadside ditches that have specific dimensions and slope to move stormwater to an outfall. Instead, the report discussed a ditch along a property line as an outfall without ever demonstrating it was intended to be one. This ditch was not indicated on the 1952 VDOT road plans, and water would have to travel an extra mile north, east, then south to reach the same outfall the roadside ditches connected to in a straight line via the special design ditches.

MPPDC Response Ignores Code of Virginia and Endorses Flawed Report

Requested a legal review of alleged errors and factual inaccuracies promoted by several constituents related to a Middle Peninsula Ditch Ownership study recently completed by John Morris of Beal, Etherington and Morris. Legal staff has reviewed the claims and has found no basis or reason to modify the findings of the study. (Lewie Lawrence, MPPDC January 2014 Meeting Packet.)

Flawed Studies Hide the Truth

A County Board of Supervisors, Commonwealth agency staff, students and the general public believe reports generated by MPPDC are factual and accurate because the sponsoring state and federal agencies have accepted them. When reports are incorrect and ignore the realities affecting Mathews County and the other five counties of the Middle Peninsula Planning District, the distribution of those reports prevents further current studies or research. Why study what's been answered?

Facts Omitted from the MPPDC Roadside and Drainage Outfall Ditches Report

FACT: As an agency of the Commonwealth, VDOT doesn't need an easement to use a natural stream for drainage if the flow is not excessive and no damage is done to the stream or its banks.

Surface water is defined in statute and regulation as "all state waters that are not ground water as defined in § 62.1-255 of the Code of Virginia." *Thus, ditches that contain and/or convey surface water are considered state waters.* (DEQ Guidance Memo No. 08-2004.)

FACT: Streams may be called ditches, but are still streams and may be used for drainage purposes.

V. Streams, Ditches, and Channelized Streams

The VWP [Virginia Water Protection] regulation makes a distinction between ditches and channelized streams. In many parts of the state, streams have been channelized and used as stormwater conveyances (i.e., streams located along roads that serve as roadside ditches and streams that serve as drainages in certain low-lying localities). These streams may colloquially be called 'ditches' even though they are actually part of the stream network. Streams that have been channelized, relocated, or incorporated into a ditch, wholly or in part, are still considered streams and are regulated as streams. (In other words, when a stream is relocated in whole or in part into a ditch, that ditch is regulated as a stream). However, it may be necessary to maintain the secondary purpose of these features (i.e., drainage). (DEQ Memo 08-2004.)

FACT: VDOT has consistently violated the provisions of the Code of Virginia by creating berms across streams and outfall ditches and by pushing piles of gravel and other debris into roadside and outfall ditches after grading, snow-plowing and mowing.

Code of Virginia §62.1-194.1. Obstructing or contaminating state waters.

Except as otherwise permitted by law, it shall be unlawful for any person to dump, place or put, or cause to be dumped, placed or put into, upon the banks of or into the channels of any state waters any object or substance, noxious or otherwise, which

may reasonably be expected to endanger, obstruct, impede,
contaminate or substantially impair the lawful use or enjoyment
of such waters and their environs by others.

FACT: VDOT is responsible for maintenance of the drainage
pipe at private entrances on highways with ditches.

Code of Virginia: 24VAC30-73-90. Private entrances.

E. Maintenance of private entrances shall be by the owner of the
entrance, except that VDOT shall maintain:

1. *On shoulder section highways, that portion of the entrance*
   within the normal shoulder portion of the highway.

2. *On highways with ditches, the drainage pipe at the entrance.*

3. *On highways with curb, gutter, and sidewalk belonging to*
   VDOT, that portion of the entrance that extends to the back
   of the sidewalk. If a sidewalk is not present, that portion of
   the entrance that extends to the back of the curb line.

4. *On highways with curb, gutter, and sidewalk not belonging to*
   VDOT, only to the flow line of the gutter pan.

5. *On highways with shoulders, ditches, and sidewalk belonging*
   to VDOT, that portion of the entrance that extends to the
   back of the sidewalk.

13

From Silviculture to Rice Paddies

V DOT'S REFUSAL TO MAINTAIN THE highway drainage system of roadside ditches, pipes and outfalls not only results in roadway deterioration, but leads to a loss of timber crops from repeated flooding of properties adjacent to those ditches.

Mathews resident David Morgan told the Board of Supervisors at the April 2014 meeting that in spite of his efforts to maintain ditches on his property, his woods are now flooded by highway runoff from blocked outfalls. As a result of the flooding, the value of recently harvested timber was reduced by $2,500 an acre from the 2012 price.

Loblolly pines are not suited to grow in flooded conditions. In marsh or swamp areas, they are found on hummocks (small areas raised above the water). The US Forest Service notes that for these pines, the "poorest performance is on shallow soils, eroded soils, and very wet or waterlogged sites. (USDA, *Silvics of North America*, 1990.)

Loblolly pine seedlings or saplings cannot withstand prolonged flooding. Complete inundation for more than 2 weeks during the growing season often results in significant mortality. Larger trees are classed as moderately tolerant of flooding; typically they can survive one season but usually succumb during the second growing season if continuously in 0.3 m (1 ft) or more of water. (USDA, Silvics of North America.)

Tree tip-over (when a tree is uprooted from saturated ground) destroys the value of that tree and any others it knocks down when it falls. Falling trees pose an additional risk of damage to homes, vehicles, and utility lines. Damage to other trees that remain standing increases the risk of diseases and insect infestations.

Mathews County has experienced an increased loss of timber from woodlands flooded by blocked outfalls and flooded roadside ditches. VDOT has ignored the fact that failure to deliver highway runoff to adequate receiving bodies of water impacts adjacent lands. By preventing normal drainage patterns, water accumulates in the woodlands. Blocked entrance and cross pipes, berms across outfalls and inadequately-sized pipes for channelized streams cause water to be dammed up in an unnatural way.

Forest Loss from Flooded Soil Damages the Environment

What happens when the soil becomes flooded? The oxygen that was present in the soil rapidly disappears, as it is used in respiration by soil microbes and roots. Replenishment of the soil oxygen from the atmosphere is inhibited because of a very slow diffusion rate in water—10,000 times less than in air. (Batzer and Sharitz, 2007.)

VDOT's failure to allow rainwater from its highways to move to receiving bodies of water threatens our air quality. Along with the loss of oxygen from trees that die, flooded soil cannot replenish its oxygen and releases greenhouse gases and other substances. Without oxygen, chemical reactions in soil release iron and manganese, and naturally occurring bacteria create greenhouse gases: methane, nitrous oxide and hydrogen sulfide (known as swamp gas or sewer gas with its pungent rotten egg odor). The Warnell School of Forest Resources in Georgia describes additional serious impacts of flooded soils on the air quality.

> In flooded soils…the gasses produced include carbon-dioxide, methane, and hydrogen. Other materials, some extremely volatile and some very toxic are produced. Examples of other materials produced by decomposition of organic material under anaerobic conditions include various hydrocarbons, alcohols, carbonyls, fatty acids, phenolic acids, sulfur compounds, acetaldehyde, and cyanogenic compounds. Many of these materials escape as gas bubbles, dissolve in the water, or float to the water surface. (Coder, 1994.)

Efforts have been made since 1980 to drain rice paddies in China at least once a year to reduce production of methane from the flooded soil. (*Nature*, 2009.)

China can drain its rice paddies annually, but in Mathews County, flooded ditches exist year-round because VDOT acts according to its own mythology that standing water in ditches is acceptable.

14

Wetlands Ecology

Wetlands Aren't Always Under Water

THE US ARMY CORPS OF Engineers (Federal Register 1982) and the EPA (Federal Register 1980) jointly define wetlands as:

> *Those areas that are inundated or saturated by surface or ground water at a frequency and duration sufficient to support, and that under normal circumstances do support, a prevalence of vegetation typically adapted for life in saturated soil conditions. Wetlands generally include swamps, marshes, bogs, and similar areas.*

In Mathews County, many of our marshes are tidal, which means they are meant to drain to the bays at low tide. Even at Onemo, one of the lowest elevations in the county, the marshes drain to bare mud and sand at low tide. A teeming population of fiddler crabs is visible whenever the tide recedes indicating a healthy and thriving ecosystem.

Although fiddler crabs have gills which they use while filter feeding, they breathe oxygen from the air and dig burrows to live in that are plugged at the opening during high tide and for winter hibernation. The burrows aerate the soil and improve growing conditions for marsh grasses. The fiddler crabs emerge at low tide to feed on bacteria, algae and plant litter, which is part of the explanation why there is no muck in the VDOT tidal ditches in the marshes that do drain with each low tide.

On the other hand, across from these same clean ditches, ditches on the upland side of the road hold standing water from blocked pipes and have accumulations of muck.

Looking further inland above the clean and well-functioning tidal ditches on the Bay side, the flow is obstructed by debris. Moving still further upland, the water is dark, and muck is present. The sound of the water moving around the obstructions attracts beavers, worsening the situation—all because of inadequate VDOT ditch maintenance, not sea level rise, not lack of elevation.

> *Surface water, ground water, floodplains, wetlands and other features do not function as separate and isolated components of the watershed, but rather as a single, integrated natural system. Disruption of any one part of this system can have long-term and far-reaching consequences on the functioning of the entire system. (FEMA. Floodplain Natural Resources and Functions)*

Chapter 9 of this FEMA Floodplains training guide cites three kinds of adverse impacts from modification of natural floodplains that lead to increased flooding. Mathews hasn't experienced two of them, the first, increased runoff from widespread clearing, wetlands destruction or urban development. The second impact, pollution loading, has not increased; if anything, it has decreased as the number of farm acres and livestock numbers in the county have declined to 11 percent of 1910 levels and as alternative septic systems have been installed.

But VDOT's roads and their neglected drainage do add to the third impact FEMA lists.

Runoff is blocked or groundwater movement is interrupted.

Allowing the natural movement of runoff and groundwater is of critical importance in lowland areas because lowlands function as discharge zones. (USGS PP1731)

In these discharge zones, rainwater usually moves through the soil to the water table which is in the surficial aquifer. Some water evaporates into the atmosphere, and some is used by plants. Some of the excess water maintains the water table, and the rest is supposed to flow to streams to maintain their base flow.

Because we are in a meteor impact crater, we don't have the same soil layers or multiple aquifers found in higher elevations outside the crater. The water table can and does rise above the ground surface in our low areas when more water accumulates than can be stored or can evaporate.

This is where intermittent and ephemeral streams come in. These streams formed in low areas of Mathews as the natural drainage paths of rainfall moving to our creeks and rivers. Intermittent streams have channels and banks and flow during the rainy season; ephemeral streams are in shallower depressions and flow briefly immediately after rainfall. They are both part of the "pre-development hydrology" urban stormwater management systems attempt to imitate.

VDOT made use of those natural drainage patterns and frequently used streams which follow the contour of the land as outfall ditches. These natural contours are the reason some ditch systems turn and change direction before reaching the receiving waters.

These intermittent and ephemeral streams are part of the wet/dry pulsing of healthy wetlands. Between periods of abundant rainfall, dry periods allow the soil to replenish its oxygenated levels, just as the ebb and flow of the tides do in marshes.

Wetland soils release phosphorus when the flooding period is prolonged.

Boers compared phosphorus release from the soil of the Mukwonago wetlands under flooded and moist conditions and documented internal eutrophication. The average concentration of phosphorus in the soil water was about four times as high under flooded than moist conditions (1.09 + 0.13 mg/L vs. 0.24 + 0.07mg/L). (University of Wisconsin-Madison Arboretum, Leaflet 7.)

(Internal eutrophication is the release of nutrients by flooded soil.)

When volumes of stormwater are trapped in VDOT roadside ditches, and blocked pipes prevent regular flow through the outfalls, several negative impacts occur:

- Vegetation overtakes the streambed because there is no scour from storm events.

- Marshes are deprived of sediment essential for their survival.

- Adjacent lands are saturated or inundated, disrupting their ecosystem.

- Downstream waters are deprived of oxygen-rich precipitation.

- Beavers attracted by sounds of obstructed flows down trees, causing more blockage.

- Cyanobacteria colonize in the ditches.

The presence of two species of cyanobacteria capable of producing toxins puts the county's children, pets, wildlife, fish and birds at risk. (Both species found in Mathews, *Microcystis aeruginosa* and *Oscillatoria,* can release microcystins—a cyanotoxin that can cause skin reactions and liver and nerve damage.)

The remedy and prevention of all these negative impacts is straight-forward: VDOT must restore the natural drainage patterns in Mathews County by opening VDOT pipes and cleaning the ditch channels.

Swales and Ditches Aren't Wetlands

Wet swales and flooded ditches are not true wetlands. They do not have the complex interactive biological system of microbes, plants and animals of true wetlands, and they cannot offer the same benefits. Because of the constant presence of standing water, they can develop wetlands vegetation, most often marsh grasses, reeds and cattails. Both wet swales and flooded ditches can have a negative impact on water quality by providing an additional source of eutrophication (the build-up of nutrients) from microbial action in constantly flooded mineral-rich soil.

If a wetland is flooded for a week or more, the soil can release phosphorus through its own chemical activity, that is, without any new influx of phosphorus from the watershed. Thus, a wetland could be harmed if a dam or other structure is installed and marsh water levels become stable. The soil would be anaerobic all the time, and it could release enough phosphorus to stimulate growth of invasive cattails. In fact, long-term observations have shown that wetlands with stabilized water levels do experience rapid expansions of cattails (Wilcox et al. 1985, Shay et al. 1999) (UW Arboretum Leaflet 7.)

Wet Swales Are Less Effective Than Dry Swales

As a stormwater management facility, wet swales are less effective than dry grassed swales for removing phosphorus, nitrogen and metals from stormwater. The Federal Highway Administration Fact Sheet on swales notes that removal of total suspended solids is the same for both wet and dry swales—between 80 and 90 percent, but there are significant differences for the other pollutants:

Amount removed by:	Dry Swales	Wet Swales
Metals	80-90 percent	40-70 percent
Total Phosphorus	65 percent	20 percent
Total Nitrogen	50 percent	40 percent

This chart does not show how much phosphorus is added to the stormwater in a wet swale. When there is standing water in wet swales, natural microbial action causes mineral-rich soils to release phosphorus once dissolved oxygen in the water is used up.

Experiments at the University of Wisconsin-Madison Arboretum with four wet swales showed the "...swale with a longer pooling period and abundant cattails, actually worsened the water quality. All three swales discharged phosphorus, and Swale III also released nitrogen and suspended solids." (Peng, 2013.)

Wet Swales Increase the Risk of Phosphorus Pollution

With the soil under a wet swale already saturated, little or no infiltration of stormwater after a heavy storm occurs, especially with the high water table in Mathews, and standing water increases. A dry swale, on the other hand, can absorb some of the precipitation as it falls.

Eutrophication (nutrient build-up) from plant growth in standing water in wet swales poses an imminent risk for the deterioration of water quality. Mathews County does not have any local waters with a phosphorus TMDL impairment, but the continued release of phosphorus from flooded soil provides an increasing reservoir of phosphorus that will eventually reach the Chesapeake Bay.

In addition to the long-term impact on water quality, the release of phosphorus stimulates increased growth of water-loving and often invasive plants which are far from ideal vegetation for stormwater management.

Some of these invasive water-dependent plants, such as cattails and phragmites, out-compete indigenous plants and dominate the area. Cattails and phragmites have rhizomes—thickened stems that grow along and under the ground and send out roots from nodes along their length. These plants take up phosphorus from flooded soil in their growing season and store it in their rhizomes and leaves. When dead leaves fall and decay, the phosphorus is released into the water and then acts as a growth stimulant, especially for cattails.

A.M. Boers 2006 dissertation at the University of Wisconsin describes the results of experiments with cattails and phosphorus.

> *Boers grew invasive cattails (T. x glauca) in microcosms at the Arboretum and showed that cattails could increase their growth when more phosphorus is available, as with internal eutrophication. First, he showed that phosphorus was limiting to cattail growth, because pots with phosphorus added had 23% more biomass of roots and shoots than those without phosphorus*

addition. Next, he showed that prolonged flooding increased both phosphorus uptake and cattail growth; that is, cattails can take up and make use of phosphorus when soils are simply flooded— without phosphorus addition from an external source.

When VDOT mows vegetation, the cuttings remain where they fall. Nitrogen and phosphorus are released into standing water as the plant material breaks down. Adding to the problem, invasive cattail rhizomes growing along the surface of the swale form dense clumps which impair the flow of stormwater and reduce the filtering capability of the swale, and mowing becomes more difficult and time-consuming.

VDOT has already allowed invasive marsh grasses to become established in the wet center of what started out as dry swales on Route 14 between the VDOT facility and Route 611 (Church Street). Based on recent history, it's likely these areas will become worse over time. VDOT mowing is already skipping over some sections of these flooded swales, just as VDOT avoids mowing sections of flooded ditches on Route 14 between the VDOT Mathews facility and North where tributaries to the East and North Rivers are unable to freely flow across the highway. There is no drainage in these ditch sections at all because of blocked pipes, ditches and incorrect slope, leaving marsh grasses in full control of constantly flooded ditches that were intended to empty in a week or less.

Cattails are rapidly spreading in the roadside ditches approaching the North River tributary crossing Route 14 near Route 660. This area is part of new VDOT road construction and indicates a failure in their current application of drainage methods and practice.

The consequences of this short-sighted behavior in allowing and constructing roadside ditches that do not drain, cannot be mowed and encourage cattail invasion may end up being catastrophic for the health and welfare of Mathews County and the Chesapeake Bay.

15

Mathews Is Still Rural

Why Mimic Rural Hydrology in a Rural Area?

Bioretention is intended to slow the passage of rainwater to streams and other waterways by capturing and allowing it to filter through a specially landscaped area. Some of the rainwater is expected to infiltrate into the ground, and the systems are generally designed to hold up to 10 inches of water. Amounts greater than this are supposed to be able to overflow or move through an underdrain into a storm drain. Bioretention does not recharge groundwater according to the EPA Rain Gardens Fact Sheet. The main function of bioretention is to help remove chemicals, excess nitrogen and phosphorus or bacteria picked up by urban runoff.

The EPA refers to bioretention as a BMP (Best Management Practice) for highly urbanized areas, useful for small hardscaped areas like parking lots. The guidelines specifically state bioretention is not appropriate for clayey areas or those with a seasonally high water table within two to five feet of the bottom of the bioretention cell.

Mathews has never been urban, and it is unlikely it ever will be. Going by the Mathews County Comprehensive Plan, except for a narrow strip along Route 626 (Ridge Road), there are no areas outside of the immediate shoreline or the extreme northwestern edge of the county where the depth to the water table comes anywhere near 2 feet or more. In fact, the depth to the seasonal high water table is listed as 6 to 15 inches for most of the county. Considering this, the use of bioretention in Mathews County would have a high risk of interaction with our groundwater supply from the surficial aquifer. Since that aquifer is also in contact with the Yorktown/Eastover aquifer in many places—the only other viable source for domestic water supplies in Mathews County, bioretention should be banned in the County.

Urban stormwater management practices do not belong in rural settings because they are meant to compensate for natural soil being covered by hard, impermeable surfaces, like asphalt or concrete, which prevent infiltration of rainfall. The rapid runoff that results from hardscaping can cause erosion and sedimentation. In an urban setting, urban runoff can pick up litter, animal waste and chemicals which must then be treated in wastewater facilities. The goal of urban stormwater BMPs is to mimic pre-development hydrology: the way precipitation moves over and is absorbed by land that has not been influenced by humans.

The level of development in Mathews, except in the central Courthouse village area, is closer to pre-development hydrology than any urban area can be. In Mathews, the woodlands and natural streams that move to larger bodies of water and wetlands are still close to pre-development hydrology and to the goal of Green Infrastructure for Linear Projects (roads). The one flaw in the system is the failure of the highway drainage system.

When rural highway drainage systems work as intended, natural patterns of precipitation, infiltration and movement to larger bodies of water are preserved. The VDOT drainage system must be restored, and the reasons why urban stormwater management do not fit Mathews must also be understood.

Rainwater Should Not Be Retained in Mathews

Retained/detained stormwater facilities concentrate pollutants as part of their intended process. To protect groundwater from the long-term accumulation of these pollutants, there must be adequate soil between the facility and the seasonally high water table. Mathews lacks sufficient depth to the water table to protect its water supply from concentrated pollutants in retention/detention facilities—pollutants like phosphorus that would remain insoluble in unflooded soil.

Mathews has no wastewater treatment plant, and no storm drains are connected to the Hampton Roads Sanitation District. The few storm drains that exist in the county drain to natural waterways.

Mathews has highly mineralized bio-active soil. Beneficial bacteria that break down plant matter to soil require oxygen. Channelized streams and outfall ditches support numerous waterways and require the natural flow of oxygenated rainwater to maintain healthy ecosystems of bacteria, plants and animals.

When stormwater is retained/detained, it loses its oxygen, and beneficial bacteria die off. Other soil microbes can survive without oxygen and release the naturally occurring minerals in the soil (iron, phosphorus, manganese, sulfur). These anaerobic bacteria produce and release methane, hydrogen sulfide and nitrous oxide—all long-lasting greenhouse gases.

Green Infrastructure in Linear Projects

The only "linear projects" in Mathews County are its roads and associated open drainage channels (ditches and channelized streams), and the forced sewer transmission line for the Hampton Roads Sanitation District from the central Courthouse village area through Gloucester. The sewer line is a closed line that has no connection to stormwater management.

Green Infrastructure (GI) are methods used to reduce the amount of stormwater runoff entering storm sewer systems that then needs to be treated in a wastewater plant. Combined storm and sewage systems can overflow during heavy storms resulting in a mixture of untreated sewage and stormwater reaching and contaminating waterways. Green Infrastructure is primarily intended for urban systems, while Mathews has no combined storm and sewage systems.

Retention/detention facilities are inappropriate for Mathews County because of the seasonally high water table. Allowing stormwater to travel along grass-lined roadside ditches to outfalls to reach streams, rivers or marshes as it would have before roads were built comes closest to the pre-development hydrology all stormwater BMPs try to replicate. The low volume of impervious surfaces that prevent infiltration of water into soil, low population density, extensive wooded areas, insignificant agricultural and livestock impacts are all in accord with the concept of Green Infrastructure.

Restoring the Mathews County drainage system carrying rainfall from roadside ditches to outfall ditches to receiving waters in a timely fashion should rank at the top of Green Infrastructure efforts.

2014 National Fish and Wildlife Foundation Grant

At 104 persons per square mile, and fewer than 9,000 residents, Mathews is far from urban (defined by the Census Bureau as a densely settled population center of at least 2,500 people). The NFWF grant study is not the first time VDOT has been connected to a project involving "green infrastructure."

The VDOT Route 14 Main Street Drainage Improvement Plan construction is being designed with a companion enhancement grant which includes rain gardens according to the preliminary design link from the Mathews Main Street website project page. (http://mathewsmainstreet.org) That page has an example of a "Rain Garden—Built Example," which shows a sign explaining how a rain garden functions.

> *Street runoff flows through curb cuts into these stormwater planters. The flow slows while plants filter and clean the stormwater, which then soaks into the ground. During very heavy rain, some water will flow back into the street and into the next stormwater planter. Water that flows out of the last planter will drain into the street inlet.*

The sidebar on the pictured sign reveals the pictured rain garden is in Portland, Oregon.

> *Portland's average rainfall of 37 inches a year generates about 10 billion gallons of stormwater runoff. If stormwater isn't properly managed, it can wash pollution into rivers and streams, cause flooding and erosion, destroy habitat and contributes to combined sewer overflows (CSOs). The City of Portland promotes stormwater management techniques that mimic natural conditions by allowing rain to filter through vegetation and soak into the ground. Green Street projects integrate stormwater*

into urban areas, improve water quality, and are attractive
neighborhood amenities.

Portland's population is over 603,000 in 133 square miles.
Mathews has fewer than 9,000 people in 86 square miles. Portland
has storm and sewage lines that can cause combined sewer
overflows that force untreated sewage into their waterways.
Mathews does not. An equally extreme difference between the
two locations is the depth to the water table. A random sampling
of Portland's depths on the USGS site ranges from 130 to 300 feet
below the surface, compared to Mathews seasonal high water table
of 6-15 inches as shown in the County's Comprehensive Plan. It is
questionable if suitable locations for rain gardens on Mathews Main
Street can be found according to VDOT's own Drainage Manual.

Depth to Water Table

Bioretention basins should not be installed on sites with a
high groundwater table. Inadequate separation between the
BMP bottom and the surface of the water table may result in
contamination of the water table. This potential contamination
arises from the inability of the soil underlying the BMP to
filter pollutants prior to their entrance into the water table.
Additionally, a high water table can flood the bioretention cell
and render it inoperable during periods of high precipitation
and/or runoff. A separation distance of no less than two feet is
required between the bottom of a bioretention basin and the
surface of the seasonally high water table. Unique site conditions
may arise which require an even greater separation distance.

Separation Distances

> *Bioretention basins should be located at least 20 feet down-slope and at least 100 feet up-slope from building foundations. Bioretention basins should not be located within 100 feet of any water supply well. Local health officials should be consulted when the implementation of a bioretention basin is proposed within the vicinity of a septic drainfield.*

> *Bioretention facilities must not be subjected to continuous or very frequent flows. Such conditions will lead to anaerobic conditions which support the export of previously captured pollutants from the facility.*

Cyanobacteria were photographed growing in rainwater in the gutter on Main Street in May 2014. There is nothing that would prevent cyanobacteria from growing in any rain gardens placed along Main Street, putting their toxins within reach of children and pets.

A best management practice for a highly urbanized area is one that has no place in a rural setting, especially not one that, to a large degree, retains the "pre-development hydrology" bioretention facilities imitate.

From Outfall Drainage Restoration to Ditch Enhancement in VDOT Right-of-Way

Mathews has a low population, large undeveloped areas and natural spaces, no major industry and no big mall. So why would the Middle Peninsula Planning District Commission team up with VDOT to obtain a grant to design ditch enhancements in the right-of-way when the County was promised a study of its outfalls which move water from one road's right-of-way to the next road's?

As discussed earlier, VDOT proposed that the Board of Supervisors in April 2013, use $15,000 of the Mathews Secondary Road Six-Year Improvement Program funds for a study on restoring outfalls in the southern end of the county. If that study had occurred, it might have provided a plan that could have been applied to the rest of the county as well. Although the two previous studies (US Corps of Engineers in 1960 and the Shore Engineering Garden Creek Watershed drainage study commissioned by Mathews County in 1980) are still valid in many ways, they need to be updated to see what changes have occurred in the past 34 to 54 years.

In October and December 2013, Sean Trapani told the Board of Supervisors the National Fish and Wildlife Foundation (NFWF) grant would cover engineering services for the drainage study. He said then the funds designated earlier in 2013 from the Secondary Six-Year Program would be used for the actual work, and revenue sharing funds could be used for the drainage project work, although the amount of the revenue sharing wasn't known yet.

The four areas chosen for the grant study were not selected on the basis of complaints to VDOT, or by impaired watersheds, or by any organized study, but by asking individual Board of Supervisors members to point out areas where there is a problem with drainage. Throwing a dart at a county map could have picked areas with an equivalent number of ditch problems because they exist everywhere—in low and high elevations—from decades of VDOT neglect and failed maintenance.

As it is, the four areas selected all have seasonally high water tables and roadside and outfall ditches unmaintained for decades, along with a significant number of blocked pipes. Draper Aden Associates, the engineering company awarded the grant is an expert in urban stormwater measures, particularly bioretention and MS4s (municipal separate storm sewer systems). This is a well-respected company in business since 1972, however, their website does not mention any rural open channel roadside and outfall ditch projects. Their focus appears to be urban stormwater systems.

> *Our stormwater experts focus on urban runoff management compliance strategies providing positive impacts to the environment, individual project economics, and long-term regulatory compliance. (Draper Aden Associates, Services)*

The Ditches of Mathews County Project asked MPPDC for a description of the scope of the NFWF grant application in April 2014. Their response was the first public confirmation that the study authorized by the Mathews Board of Supervisors a year earlier had been changed from a county-wide outfall drainage restoration study to one that would help VDOT decide how to use its "limited funding for construction of ditch improvement projects within public rights-of-way."

Project Abstract:

> *Through collaboration with MPPDC, Mathews County, the Virginia Department of Transportation (VDOT), and a Rural Ditching Committee comprised of citizens of Mathews County, Draper Aden Associates proposes to identify potential causes and remedies to improve existing issues and water quality within Mathews County. VDOT currently has limited funding for construction of ditch improvement projects within public rights-of-way; VDOT will use the information gathered as part of this study to determine the best use of the available funding for implementation.*

*Outcome of the project will be that Mathews County can
provide recommendations to its private citizens and VDOT
for improvements to the ditch system, including increasing
conveyance of stormwater and improving water quality in
Mathews County. The results of the study will be transferrable to
other counties within the region.*

Mathews County's Role:

*Mathews County will be a project partner that will provide
local guidance and oversight to this project. Mathews County
Administration will create a local Rural Ditching Committee
by facilitating appointments to serve on this committee. The
Administrator may seek a Board appointed or administratively
appointed committee. The Rural Ditching Committee will consist
of Mathews County citizens living within drainage problem
areas identified by the Mathews County Board of Supervisors.
The Rural Ditching Committee will provide a focused avenue for
public involvement and education.*

VDOT Myths Influence NFWF Grant Proposal

A copy of the full grant proposal, though, revealed a slightly
different emphasis. Lewis Lawrence, MPPDC Executive Director,
incorrectly blamed "poorly draining soils, a high water table, and
topographic constraints" for standing water in ditches, and stated,
"Additionally, the majority of the ditches and adjacent areas are turf
grass and are frequently mowed further reducing the capacity of the
ditches and culverts."

The first point: poorly draining soils, shows a complete lack of
understanding of the geology behind our rural ditches. The ditches
were located so that they were cut in clay layers that would not

wash away or add excess sediment to the stormwater flow. Once the ditch line is established, the clay layer is stable and doesn't react to the presence or absence of water as silty soils do. Because of this clay layer, the water table, even in the wettest weather, does not drain to the ditches. Channelized streams, however, continue to flow to their natural watershed outlet unless blocked and may carry flow from the surficial (groundwater) aquifer. This is a natural function of intermittent streams in watershed discharge zones near the Chesapeake Bay.

The second point: topographic constraints, is another way of repeating the VDOT myth that Mathews is too flat to drain. If ditch obstructions and debris are removed, and the slope is correct within the ditch, water will not stand, it will flow—as long as the pipes or outfall are not blocked.

The third point makes no sense: "...the majority of the ditches and adjacent areas are turf grass and are frequently mowed further reducing the capacity of the ditches and culverts." Perhaps Mr. Lawrence intended to say, "infrequently mowed," which would be a true statement, but probably not, given that the other three points are not why VDOT's roadside ditches don't drain. Grass-lined ditches were one of the earliest forms of natural biofiltration. Short, dense turf grass slowed the flow of rainwater enough to allow sediment to drop out of the flow and absorbed small amounts of water left in the ditch after a rain. Grass performs the same function in stormwater management dry swales; it slows the rainwater flow, causes sediment to drop and be trapped, uses some of the water to sustain itself and gives off oxygen. In addition, the root structure adds stability to the soil, preventing erosion.

The Ditches of Mathews County Says VDOT Is Responsible for VDOT Ditch Failure

Another grant proposal statement claims the Ditches of Mathews County Facebook page is about the citizens' concern with "improving the adequacy of ditches and who is ultimately responsible for managing and improving the ditches." To the contrary, The Ditches of Mathews County has no question that VDOT is responsible for the VDOT ditches' failure.

> *The Ditches of Mathews County once were an effective stormwater management system for the roads. Mathews County has unique features and challenges. VDOT neglect causing road damage should not be one of them.*
>
> *One of the few places in the world entirely inside a meteor impact crater, Mathews County has a relatively low, flat topography. Roadways here act like dams, preventing the natural flow of rainwater to our waterways. Roadside ditches are supposed to gather the water from the roads and conduct it to "adequate receiving channels" (larger ditches connecting the roadside ditches to our rivers, creeks, bays and marshes). This is intended to do two things: prevent damage to the roadbed and prevent flooding and damage of adjacent properties. VDOT's deferred or neglected maintenance of the roadside ditch system and related outfalls is causing widespread failure of the system and damage. It's time to get our ditches working again and let them carry fresh, oxygenated water once more. (Facebook, The Ditches of Mathews County.)*

VDOT's interest in this study's outcome is framed in terms of construction, without a word about their failed maintenance policies.

The specific points made in the grant application are:

A. A plan and profile sketch of existing and proposed conditions;

B. A typical 'strategy' cross-section for existing and proposed conditions, depicting recommendations for grading and landscaping;

C. Maintenance recommendations;

D. A summary of preliminary opinion of probable construction costs and estimated pollutant removal;

E. Summary of definition of responsible parties;

F. Recommendations for implementation.

To restore VDOT ditches in Mathews County does not require landscaping. Landscaping cannot increase conveyance of stormwater through outfalls obstructed by trees and storms or through pipes blocked by decades without maintenance.

Item D includes providing an estimate of pollutant removal; this implies knowledge of what pollutants exist in fresh rainwater. In a way, that makes sense. If the ditches function, fresh rainwater is not polluted, but 90% of nothing, is still nothing. So no matter what improvement the report says the planned stormwater facilities will produce, the true result is likely to be none.

All of the current negative impacts to stormwater are not related to runoff; they are a direct result of lack of natural flow to receiving waters.

- Loss of oxygen from rainwater by impounding in blocked ditches.

- Cyanobacterial mats further block flow and release of toxins when cells are damaged or die.

- Invasive cattails with rhizomes that pull more phosphorus that stimulates cattail growth.

- Release of phosphorus from soil that's flooded and from cattails that drop dead leaves in fall.

- Development of muck from deoxygenation of water and loss of beneficial bacteria.

- Flooding of adjacent properties and woods and subsequent property damage and timber loss.

NFWF Grant-related Education

Another part of the NFWF 2014 grant plan is to "educate" the committee members on stormwater, water quality, TMDLs and green infrastructure so they can in turn "educate" other residents. Since most green infrastructure is aimed at reducing the impact of urban settings, and the Mathews study areas are rural, this should be an opportunity to explore rural alternatives to maintain an already green infrastructure of extensive forests, low density development and clean air.

As for "incorporating education of stormwater, water quality, TMDLs, and green infrastructure—key elements of this study," the citizens on the grant Stormwater Ditch Steering Committee will be prepared to share their practical knowledge and expertise on ditches and local drainage issues.

The grant proposal asserts that 0 people have been "reached by outreach, training, or technical assistance activities" and that the grant will result in 200 people reached. Contrary to that statement, at least that many people have been reached in the past two years as a result of the Piankatank, Milford Haven, Gwynn's Island TMDL Implementation Plan meetings with DCR/DEQ, personal contacts with TMDL working group members, Facebook and *Inside the Crater* blog posts. There were 5 Mathews residents at a DEQ water testing training program in 2014, and several more plan to take the class.

Chesapeake Style magazine has published a column, "The Ditches of Mathews County," since September 2012. The magazine distributes 10,000-12,000 copies through the Northern Neck, Middle Peninsula and Williamsburg. It's likely more than 200 people have read the columns and learned something from them about drainage in Mathews County, VDOT activities, Total Maximum Daily Loads and water quality.

Will Draper Aden Associates take this opportunity to work with local residents to develop a plan that makes sense and will restore the drainage functions of our VDOT roadside and outfall ditches? Or will they recommend urban stormwater management practices that will destroy what's left of Mathews County's rural highway drainage system?

Rainwater Doesn't Need Water Quality Improvement

Mathews County residents have been good stewards of their land for centuries. Freshly fallen rainwater needs to travel from ditches to receiving bodies of water instead of being held captive until it's out of oxygen and full of muck. This oxygenated rain would help our waters recover their natural ecosystems, and those beneficial bacteria, plants, animals, fish and shellfish could maintain these conditions if they continue to have enough oxygen to thrive and water clarity for sunlight to destroy *E. coli* bacteria.

The marshes need the regular flow from uplands to bring the sediments that allow the natural process of fiddler crabs eating bacteria, algae and bits of vegetative debris. When the fiddler crabs excrete the cleaned grains of sand with their mucus, they begin the soil building process. When they dig burrows, they aerate the soil and bring oxygen to the roots of marsh grasses, allowing those roots to grow deeper and nourish and support the grasses. Other bacteria and microscopic animals have a niche in this ecosystem and play a part in the food chain.

The future of our waters depends on the recognition that the health of our marshes, creeks, rivers, smaller bays and the Chesapeake Bay itself is connected to the restoration of the outfall ditches and the entire highway drainage system in Mathews County.

16

Bioretention or Biohazard?

Mosquitoes, Microcystins and Muck

WHEN NATURAL RAINWATER FLOW IN Mathews County watersheds is blocked, public health risks increase from mosquitoes, microcystins and muck.

Mosquitoes

VDOT's history of roadside and outfall ditch maintenance failure has reached crisis proportions and increased the risk of mosquito-borne disease.

Mosquitoes can hatch in even a teaspoon of still water. When thousands of acres of woodlands are flooded by blocked VDOT drainage ditches, the possible numbers of mosquitoes are beyond counting. Snapping turtles, bats, frogs and birds feed on some of them, but unfortunately, they can't eat enough to control entire mosquito populations.

Mosquitoes pick up the West Nile virus and Eastern equine encephalitis virus by feeding on birds infected with the virus. While only a small percentage of mosquitoes carry the virus, and an equally small number of humans who are bitten get infected by West Nile virus, this is of little comfort to the 50 percent of Mathews residents who are over 50 and at greater risk of severe illness should they contract it, according to the Virginia Department of Health West Nile virus fact sheet.

The Virginia Department of Health states in their Eastern equine encephalitis virus (EEEV) fact sheet that people over 50 and under 15 are at greater risk for developing severe disease from West Nile virus. Human cases are rare, but "about 35 percent of people who develop the disease die. It is estimated that 35 percent of people who survive EEEV will have mild to severe neurologic aftereffects from this disease."

The arrival of another mosquito-borne virus in the United States, CHIKV (Chikungunya virus), adds a new level of risk. The risk is high, especially considering the CDC reported the first cases appeared in late 2013 in some Caribbean countries, and by September 19, 2014, there were 729,178 suspected and 10,845 laboratory-confirmed cases in 34 countries or territories in the Caribbean, Central America, South America or North America.

The Center for Disease Control reported the number of cases rose from only a handful of travel-related cases in Florida in May 2014 to 37 in 10 states by June 10 and escalated to 1,125 cases in 46 states by September 23, 2014, with 25 travel-related cases in Virginia. *Aedes aegypti* and *Aedes albopictus* mosquitoes, both of which are found in Virginia, carry CHIKV.

As of July 1, there were no locally transmitted cases in the continental US, but as of September 23, 11 locally-transmitted cases were reported from Florida and 418 laboratory-confirmed cases had occurred in Puerto Rico and 45 in the US Virgin Islands.

An article in the Journal of Virology, states, "...local authorities should immediately pursue and reinforce epidemiological and entomological surveillance to avoid a severe epidemic." (Vega-Rua, et al, 2014.)

Although the Fact Sheet on Stormwater Management and Vector Breeding Habitats from the National Center for Environmental Health doesn't address CHIKV, the same principles apply as for West Nile virus and Saint Louis encephalitis virus.

Stormwater management regulations and practices developed by environmental management agencies address the environmental problem of sediments and other pollutants entering surface waters but do not address public health issues, such as preventing habitat production for disease-carrying mosquitoes and other vectors.

Certain stormwater management structures designed to reduce sediment and other pollutant loads in runoff (e.g., dry detention basins, retention ponds, media filtration devices, below-ground devices) frequently hold standing water for more than 3 days, creating potential mosquito breeding habitats. This in turn leads to the potential for mosquito-borne diseases such as West Nile virus and St. Louis encephalitis.

Even those stormwater facilities that are properly designed and constructed to minimize mosquito breeding habitat may collect standing water if they are not maintained properly, thus creating the potential for mosquito breeding.

*Properly design and construct stormwater control structures
(especially regarding slopes, pipe inverts, and volumes) to
minimize the inadvertent creation of standing water. Water
should be held less than 72 hours whenever possible (shorter than
minimum mosquito- breeding time).*

Mosquitoes are not the only health risk from drainage features that stay flooded for extended periods. Wet swales and flooded ditches pose additional risks to the community by providing habitat for cyanobacteria which produce microcystins and other toxins.

Cyanobacteria

*Cyanobacteria are one of the earth's most ancient life forms.
Evidence of their existence on earth, derived from fossil records,
encompasses a period of some 3.5 billion years in the late
Precambrian era. Cyanobacteria are the dominant phytoplankton
group in eutrophic freshwater bodies worldwide. They have
caused animal poisoning in many parts of the world and may
present risks to human health through drinking and recreational
activity. Cyanobacteria produce two main groups of toxin,
namely neurotoxins and peptide hepatotoxins. (Oberholster,
2004.)*

Many cyanobacteria (blue-green algae) species release toxins when their cells are damaged or die. There is no way to identify toxin-producers, other than genetic testing. These cyanotoxins can affect dogs, wildlife, birds, fish and humans.

Cyanobacteria can be found in the most diverse environments like hot springs, salt marshes, soils, fresh, brackish, and marine waters [Sze, 1986].

Cyanotoxins are usually classified according to their target in mammals, being divided in hepatotoxins (liver damaging), neurotoxins (nerve damaging), cytotoxins (cell damaging) and toxins responsible for allergenic reactions (dermatotoxins). (Churro. Risk Assessment of Cyanobacteria and Cyanotoxins. 2012).

The same source indicates that some of these cyanobacteria occur in low nutrient waters and form blooms that can survive for years. Ditches of Mathews County photos verify cyanobacteria reblooming in the same VDOT roadside ditches throughout Mathews County wherever there is standing water.

In April 2013, after noticing a massive bloom of cyanobacteria in one ditch near the Courthouse area, the author took a water sample to the Virginia Institute of Marine Science. Their tests identified the cyanobacteria as *Oscillatoria*, and they measured a low level of microcystins, a cyanotoxin, at 0.270 micrograms/liter in the sample. In April 2014, VIMS again tested water samples from the ditches and did not detect microcystins, but did identify two kinds of cyanobacteria capable of producing cyanotoxins—*Oscillatoria* and *Microcystis aeruginosa*.

Microcystins may promote liver and colorectal cancer in humans according to scientific studies reviewed by Meneely in *Biomarkers*, 2013.) The journal article says "No methods exist for the determination of chronic exposure to microcystins."

Cyanotoxin Linked to Degenerative Brain Disorders

If the cancer risk of cyanotoxins isn't enough to press for action, the link of another cyanotoxin to Alzheimer's Disease and other degenerative brain diseases should be.

The cyanotoxin, BMAA (beta-N-methlyamino-L-alanine), is produced by a number of cyanobacteria. A 2012 paper published in *Environmental Health Perspectives* explores the links between BMAA and ALS (Lou Gehrig's disease—amyotrophic lateral sclerosis), Alzheimer's disease, Lewy Body Dementia, and Parkinson's disease. (Holtcamp, 2012.) This toxin crosses the blood-brain barrier and can accumulate over a period of years in brain tissue of genetically susceptible individuals, causing the neuron-tangling conditions that afflict a growing number of older Americans. According to the Alzheimer's Association, Alzheimer's is the sixth-leading cause of death in the United States.

Eliminate Standing Water to Stop Cyanobacteria

There is no treatment available to eliminate cyanobacteria in standing surface water. Using chemicals to kill the cyanobacteria releases their toxins, and the chemicals may be harmful to the environment. There is evidence, however, that natural filtering through sediments, together with denitrifying bacteria, will break down the toxins. (Holst et al, 2003.) If this proves to be the case, we are fortunate to be on well water; unlike the 400,000 people in Toledo, Ohio, and another 30,000 in Michigan, where, from August 2 to 4, 2014, residents were alerted to not drink or use city water for bathing because of high levels of microcystins.

Cyanobacteria (harmful blue-green algae) thrive in still water, not actively flowing water. If ditches drained and dried between storms, and old bacterial mats were scraped out, rainwater moving through the ditches would help keep the ditches clear of these toxin-producers. It is not possible to test every ditch in the county for toxins from cyanobacteria, but it is possible to get the water moving again and eliminate the risks to our pets and wildlife, our food chain and public health.

E. coli from Flooded Woods

Traditionally, Mathews County's roadside ditches were lined with well-established grass which caught sediment and prevented most of it from reaching the receiving waters at the end of the outfall streams and ditches. As previously discussed, some sediment is necessary to maintain our river life and marshes which is why other filtering materials have never been considered for use in our ditches. The action of grass-lined ditches with fresh oxygenated rainwater freely flowing to receiving waters is close to the pre-development hydrology urban stormwater management attempts to mimic in urban settings.

The entire system is bypassed when overgrowth of vegetation in the ditches or blockages from ditch bank failures or accidents or blocked pipes cause stormwater to back up into wooded areas instead of reaching the receiving waters through the normal outfall channels. Channelized year-round and intermittent streams have their own natural flow in addition to rainfall and will overflow their banks into the woods if their outlets are blocked.

This overland flow into wooded areas creates the very real hazard of picking up wildlife waste and forcing it into the creeks, rivers and bays. Forest wildlife do not defecate in waterways; they use the woods. Raccoons and beavers and otters often use communal latrines to mark their territorial boundaries. The CDC has a fact sheet, *Raccoon Latrines: Identification and Clean-up*. It lists areas raccoons use for latrines around homes like decks, patios, attics and garages, but the primary areas are trees (around the base and at forks) and raised horizontal surfaces like fallen logs, stumps or woodpiles. There is no question that water overflowing a stream bank and running past the base of a tree with such a latrine can push its contents to a waterway and carry *E. coli* with it.

Muck supports E. coli

Where pipes are blocked, the water level in the ditch must rise above the now-typical 50-75% blockage in the pipes in order to leave the ditch. But while the water is trapped, it rapidly loses oxygen, bringing decomposition to a halt. This leads to the creation of muck—a black smelly mass of partially decomposed plant matter. VDOT adds to the natural leaf litter that falls into ditches every time they mow and leave the cuttings in the standing water in the ditches.

> *The accumulated organic matter and associated nutrients*
> *promote two basic features of wetland ecosystems, namely*
> *an anoxic, reducing habitat of vigorously growing microbial*
> *communities, on and within the sediments and organic debris,*
> *and very actively growing aquatic plants that are adapted to these*
> *growth conditions. (Batzer. Ecology of Freshwater and Estuarine*
> *Wetlands, 2007.)*

Outfall ditches and streams develop muck in areas where the flow isn't adequate to maintain a clear stream or ditch bed because the stormwater that should provide the flow is trapped in roadside or outfall ditches. But when heavy storms come, some of the mucky sediments are pushed along to our creeks and rivers and those sediments add to our water quality impairments.

Muck interferes with the small and microscopic life forms that would usually live in the streams by lowering the oxygen levels. Except for viruses and a few bacteria like *E. coli*, most living things require oxygen for their survival, including beneficial bacteria.

Mucky sediments increase the turbidity or cloudiness of the waterways. Stirred up by rain and wind and tide change, these sediments prevent sunlight from reaching subaqueous vegetation and coat leaves, reducing the ability to use light for photosynthesis and the production of oxygen. Blocking sunlight also helps *E. coli* survive longer because the ultraviolet radiation of the sun cannot kill off the bacteria as it does in clear waters. The carbon present in the muck also provides a food source for the *E. coli* bacteria.

A study reported in the *Journal of Environmental Management* (Semenov 2009) showed *E. coli* in manure survived six months in anaerobic conditions (without oxygen), but it only survived two weeks when oxygen was present. Even though water testing may not show culturable *E. coli*, the bacteria may be present, but dormant, waiting until sediments are stirred up and nutrients become more available. (This condition is called viable, but non-culturable.) This ability to endure until nutrition is available may be part of the explanation for higher test levels of *E. coli* in our waters immediately after a storm.

E. coli Can Survive for Months Outside a Living Host

Studies over the last 7 years show that *E. coli* does not require a human or animal host to survive for extended periods. Studies in Michigan showed *E. coli* can survive 5 months in water as long as the temperature is above 39 degrees Fahrenheit. (Kashian, 2010).

Our average water temperature only goes below 39F in January and February. Based on scientific findings across the country and in Europe, naturalized *E. coli* is the most likely major source of the ongoing high bacterial readings where there is no evidence of obvious new contamination.

When wind and storms stir up sediment and release bacteria back into the water column, bottom feeding fish like spot and croaker can take in *E. coli* with whatever they're eating and become carriers. (Hansen, 2008). When birds eat those fish, the bacteria multiply and are released in the bird's droppings, in addition to what the fish excrete themselves as carriers.

If rainfall traveled through the ditch system to the receiving waters while still oxygenated, water clarity would improve because beneficial bacteria that are predators of *E. coli* could be re-established; waters would have greater clarity allowing more UV rays from the sun to reach and kill *E. coli* bacteria.

Restoring the drainage function of roadside and outfall ditches would eliminate the public health risks. Why isn't maintaining the flow out of the ditches a top public health goal?

17

Drowning a County

How Did It Happen?

GARDEN CREEK JETTIES FROM 1930S through 1960s interrupted sand movement to the south along the Chesapeake Bay coastline leading to the Winter Harbor barrier beach breach.

Sand removal from Haven Beach for highway and building construction in the 1940s decreased the volume of sand available to maintain the Winter Harbor barrier beach.

VIMS documented Mathews County shoreline changes since 1939, but there seems to be no record of calls for action to prevent the breach of the Winter Harbor barrier beach near the Garden Creek Canal before it happened or restore it afterwards.

Mathews County, VIMS, VDOT and other state agencies failed to act on the 1960 recommendations of the US Army Corps of Engineers "to improve the drainage system and encourage the preservation and rehabilitation of the barrier beach along the Chesapeake Bay."

Mathews County and VDOT ignored the 1980 Garden Creek drainage report recommendations to clean the VDOT pipes and ditches and check their elevation to ensure drainage of all areas of the Garden Creek Watershed 5 feet or more above mean sea level.

Starting around 1993, VDOT created institutional myths that prevented proper ditch maintenance and excused failure to provide maintenance by repeating incorrect statements until they became common belief.

County supervisors misinformed by VDOT and MPPDC accepted inaccurate statements as fact without challenging them.

A line of County administrators accepted VDOT's statements without question or further research, and in turn, reinforced bad information to the Supervisors over many years.

Neither the Board of Supervisors nor the Commonwealth Transportation Board required adequate and accurate financial and factual reporting on County/VDOT Revenue Sharing projects.

Lack of oversight and evaluation of the results of the 1993 to 2006 VDOT revenue sharing projects perpetuated the same failing process in Mathews County.

The Virginia Department of Health is still unable to track and report on actual numbers of septic system failures, repairs and responses by watershed, which disguises the role of failed VDOT drainage in TMDL impairments.

The Virginia Department of Health and Department of Environmental Quality focus primarily on septic system and pet waste contamination while ignoring toxic cyanobacteria in flooded VDOT ditches throughout the county and the role of those ditches in oxygen impairments in rivers and bays.

The inability of Commonwealth agencies to recognize or act on streams impaired by past VDOT practices leads to continuing degradation of the streams and highway drainage failure.

County residents worn down by the fight gave up trying to get maintenance to correct VDOT drainage failures.

Working with VIMS, the US Army Corps of Engineers built up the south side of the Winter Harbor breach to increase the dunes by depositing dredge spoils without putting any spoils to the north where sand could move southward by natural action and help heal the breach.

Commonwealth of Virginia agencies failed as stewards of the National Hydrography Dataset.

Both federal and Commonwealth mapping resources contain historical artifacts and other errors which the state has not acted to correct.

After VDOT was advised of the historical map artifacts in 2012 and 2014, VDOT insisted their calculation of the drainage area of the Mathews Main Street Drainage Improvement Project based on those artifacts was correct.

VDOT has no accessible list or map of outfall drainage easements it is supposed to maintain.

VDOT lost their 1993 outfall ditch inventory and has no clear mapping of watershed drainage patterns, so they have no way to identify where the natural drainage patterns should go and whether roadside pipes and ditches were installed at the proper slope to achieve that drainage.

There is no state agency that looks at the 'big picture' and the impacts of VDOT drainage failures.

New Legislation Could Make a Difference

When the Commonwealth constructs a road or takes one into its system, the Department of Transportation holds the responsibility for ensuring the road is capable of the proper disposition of stormwater associated with that road.

For new or revised road construction, drainage design details are recorded on road plans. For the Rural Rustic Road Program, even though there are no new plans drawn, the *Rural Rustic Program Manual* states appropriate environmental and hydraulics technical staff evaluate each project.

Legislation must spell out what anyone with common sense realizes: stormwater collected from rural roads needs a way to get to an adequate body of water, one which would have received the natural runoff if the roads didn't exist. Dumping stormwater onto public or private land without a way for it to reach a receiving body of water cannot be an option.

When the School Board of Mathews County granted a 130-foot drainage easement for a pipe taking stormwater from the opposite side of the road, no one intended for that stormwater to end up on the school's ball field or in the adjacent park. A courthouse search of the State Highway Plat Book plans showed the 130-foot easement and a dot-dashed line indicating a previous permanent easement, but the plan sheet had no reference to the date or project number. (State Highway Plat Book 3, page 211.)

VDOT staff in Saluda were unaware of even the first easement, much less the second because there is no mechanism for VDOT to track deeds and easements over time. This must be changed by enforced policy or by legislation.

VDOT has refused to follow their own manuals and guidelines for drainage and maintenance of drainage systems. Neither an individual nor a county bears the responsibility for properly channeling the stormwater from the Commonwealth's roads to Commonwealth waters.

Legislation requiring VDOT to move stormwater from roadside ditches in rural areas to an adequate receiving body of water is needed, along with a deadline for implementation by the Commonwealth Transportation Board. A simple statement, if enacted, could result in carrying out the intention of the state highway system designers to provide well-drained roadways that don't impact adjacent properties and don't suffer premature roadbed failure from poor drainage:

> The Virginia Department of Transportation (VDOT) shall
> maintain suitable outlets to adequate receiving bodies of
> water from VDOT rural open stormwater drainage ditches

receiving stormwater from rural Commonwealth primary and secondary roads.

The state does not tolerate an individual's actions if those actions endanger the health and welfare of other citizens. Citizens should not have to endure the threat to their collective health, safety and welfare from the improper and negligent behavior of state's agencies in handling stormwater from the Commonwealth's highway system.

18

It's Time for Common Sense

Highway drainage is a connected system, not isolated pieces. All aspects must work together to allow fresh stormwater to reach the creeks, rivers and bays that need it. This is the essence of emulating pre-development hydrology in stormwater management, and this is where VDOT has failed in managing its highway drainage.

The 1872 NOAA navigation chart from the Historical Map and Chart Collection (http://historicalcharts.noaa.gov/historicals/preview/image/cp707c) shows clear patterns of roads, and drainage, between parcels of land. We know from modern topographic maps, these roads followed the lay of the land. Landowners of that time had no choice but to accommodate natural watershed drainage patterns.

Modern technology allowed the Commonwealth's highway department to straighten out curves and take a road directly from one point to another—but at the expense of natural drainage through streams. Early on, engineers recognized this and tried to compensate for interrupting those streams with special design ditches and crosspipes installed under the roads at every low point. Culverts carried larger streams under the roads. These features require ongoing maintenance, and they haven't received it.

When wars and economic disasters impacted state budgets, no one intended cutbacks in maintenance to destroy our infrastructure. Yet that is the bottom line of what has happened and is happening in Mathews County. Lack of foresight in preserving road plans, failure to develop a system to track and retrieve asset records of deeds and easements, and the loss of historical knowledge of drainage patterns added to the ongoing failure and destruction.

Mathews County survived four centuries and more as a relative paradise because the people living here have valued the land, air and water around them.

Roads are a necessity of modern life, and roadside drainage must function for roads to be safe, stable and long-lasting. It's common sense to preserve road functionality and longevity.

It's common sense to eliminate the health hazards of flooded ditches, and it's environmental good sense to eliminate flooded ditch situations that lead to the degradation of healthy ecosystems. If common sense isn't enough, the Clean Water Act requires us to control factors that impair water quality in the Chesapeake Bay and its tributaries. Adequate oxygen, reasonable pH, clarity and control of harmful bacteria in our waters are all dependent on a well-functioning highway drainage system.

Throughout this book, one statement stands out time and again: the VDOT roadside ditches and pipes must be cleaned and the outfalls opened to allow rainfall to reach receiving waters. The benefits are undeniable.

- Risks to public health from mosquito-borne disease and cyanobacteria will be reduced.

- Private property will not be damaged by flooding from ditches.

- Oxygenated water will improve the quality of the receiving waters.

- Clearer waters will let sunlight kill more *E. coli* bacteria.

- Marshes will receive enough sediment to be able to survive sea level rise.

- Forests will no longer be inundated and can flourish again.

The risks of continued failure to act are unacceptable.

VDOT urban myths have no place in rural highway drainage. We can't afford to wait. It's time to get the ditches in Mathews working again, and stop Drowning a County.

Appendix A
Ditch Basics

Hydraulics

Ditches rely on the basic principles of hydraulics to move water from the roadside to receiving bodies of water. Gravity causes the water to move following the slope of the ditch. The size, shape and roughness of the ditch affect the speed at which the water moves. When any of these factors are out of sync with the others, the flow is affected.

Slope

The land in Mathews has gentle slopes except at the far northwestern end of the county where there are some ravines with 10-30 foot drops at banks along major creeks or the Piankatank River. Everywhere else, the land runs in slight contours toward the bays or rivers within each watershed. These contours are not always obvious because the slope is shallow, and they rarely run in a straight line.

Culverts

Culverts are pipes or concrete structures that carry water flow under roads, driveways or other obstructions.

Pipes

Corrugated metal or concrete pipes used before the current plastic pipes came into use are still in place throughout Mathews County. Most of the corrugated metal pipes and some of the concrete pipes are near the end of their serviceable life.

Flared sections of one concrete section are fitted over the straight end of the next pipe to make the necessary lengths.

Plastic pipe is used as a single piece, eliminating the problem of separation and leakage found in the concrete pipes which could undermine the roadway. Pipe size must be carefully calculated to allow proper flow.

Use of Streams as Outfalls

Natural streams, whether year-round, intermittent or ephemeral, follow the lay of the land. Intermittent streams only flow when the groundwater level rises high enough to emerge above the ground's surface. Ephemerals carry surface water immediately after rainfall. The natural drainage patterns of these streams were used as drainage outfalls from roadside ditches. In some cases, straight-line ditches were dug between roads to connect to natural streams and flowed in one direction throughout their entire length. Others made turns or curved following land contours. In either case, the flow moved to a natural body of water like a creek, river or bay.

Channel Revisions and Channelized Streams

Streams, especially those utilized as outfalls, are directed through pipes or concrete culverts to cross under the roads. To accommodate the flow from roadside ditches in addition to the natural stream flow, some streams were excavated and widened or straightened by VDOT or by its earlier counterpart, the Department of Highways. The North

River was straightened and channelized near Trinity Church at Route 626 before it crosses under Route 14. Both the North River, East River and Queens Creek have tributaries or headwaters that must travel under roads in more than one location. There are also many instances of smaller streams which were channelized under roads on topo maps and VDOT road plans.

Grass-Lined Ditches

Grass growing in the channels of ditches was the first mechanism used for stormwater management. The Mowing Practices section of VDOT's Best Practices Manual calls for a mowing height range of 2-4 inches for warm season grass and 4-6 inches for cool season. This was intended to create an even layer of grass to help control the rate of flow and prevent erosion within the ditches and to allow some of the sediment to fall out of the flow and settle into the grass rather than being carried to the receiving waters. The grass itself would take up some of the water in its growth cycle so that no water would remain in the ditch more than 2-3 days. Areas inadvertently mowed to a lower height or scalped (cut down to bare soil) were to be revegetated according to Road and Bridge Specifications.

Topographic Maps and Ditches

Water doesn't run uphill. In looking at topo maps, it's necessary to consider the elevation to know which way ditches flow. Ditches may appear as road-to-road on maps, but actually flow in opposite directions from a higher central point in the terrain. An example of this can be seen in the network of streams and ditches running between the East River to the south and Miller Cove off Queens Creek to the north, between Route 14 (John Clayton Memorial Highway) and Route 198 (Buckley Hall Road). Only the major branching tributaries appear on the 1965 USGS topographic map of Mathews. Ephemeral streams (smaller branches that only flow after storms depending on how wet or dry the soil is) may not appear on topo maps, but they can be essential to drainage.

Appendix B
Code of Virginia References

CODE OF VIRGINIA

§ 33.1-23.05

C. ...Any project having funds allocated under this program shall be initiated in such a fashion where at least a portion of such funds have been expended within one year of allocation. Any revenue-sharing funds for projects not initiated after two subsequent fiscal years of allocation may be reallocated at the discretion of the Commonwealth Transportation Board.

§ 33.1-69. Control, supervision and management.

A. The control, supervision, management and jurisdiction over the secondary system of state highways shall be vested in the Department of Transportation and the maintenance and improvement, including construction and reconstruction, of such secondary system of state highways shall be by the Commonwealth under the supervision of the Commissioner of Highways. The boards of supervisors or other governing bodies of the several counties and the county road board or county road commission of any county operating under a county road board or county road commission shall have no control, supervision, management and jurisdiction over such public roads, causeways, bridges, landings and wharves, constituting the secondary system of state highways.

Except as otherwise provided in this article, the Commonwealth Transportation Board shall be vested with the same powers, control and jurisdiction over the secondary system of state highways in the several counties and towns of the Commonwealth, and such additions as may be made from time to time, as were vested in the boards of supervisors or other governing bodies of the several counties or in the county road board or county road commission in any county operating under a county road board or county road commission on June 21, 1932, and in addition thereto shall be vested with the same power, authority and control as to the secondary system of state highways as is vested in the Board in connection with the State Highway System.

B. Nothing in this chapter shall be construed as requiring the Department, when undertaking improvements to any state secondary highway system component or any portion of any such component, to fully reconstruct such component or portion thereof to bring it into compliance with all design and engineering standards that would be applicable to such component or portion thereof if the project involved new construction.

§ 33.1-223.2:4. Department to maintain drainage easements

Whenever, in connection with or as a precondition to the construction or reconstruction of any highway, the Department shall have acquired any permanent drainage easement, the Department shall, until such time as such easement shall have been terminated, perform repairs required to protect the roadway and to ensure the proper function of the easement within the right-of-way and within the boundaries of such easement.

§ 62.1-10. Definitions.

As used in this chapter, the following terms shall have the meanings respectively ascribed to them:

(a) "Water" includes all waters, on the surface and under the ground, wholly or partially within or bordering the Commonwealth or within its jurisdiction and which affect the public welfare.

(b) "Beneficial use" means both instream and offstream uses. Instream beneficial uses include, but are not limited to, the protection of fish and wildlife habitat, maintenance of waste assimilation, recreation, navigation, and cultural and aesthetic values. Offstream beneficial uses include, but are not limited to, domestic (including public water supply), agricultural, electric power generation, commercial and industrial uses. Public water supply uses for human consumption shall be considered the highest priority.

§ 62.1-11. Waters declared natural resource; state regulation and conservation; limitations upon right to use.

A. Such waters are a natural resource which should be regulated by the Commonwealth.

B. The regulation, control, development and use of waters for all purposes beneficial to the public are within the jurisdiction of the Commonwealth which in the exercise of its police powers may establish measures to effectuate the proper and comprehensive utilization and protection of such waters.

C. The changing wants and needs of the people of the Commonwealth may require the water resources of the Commonwealth to be put to uses beneficial to the public to the extent of which they are reasonably capable; the waste or unreasonable use or unreasonable method of use of water should be prevented; and the conservation of such water is to be exercised with a view to the welfare of the people of the Commonwealth and their interest in the reasonable and beneficial use thereof.

D. The public welfare and interest of the people of the Commonwealth require the proper development, wise use, conservation and protection of water resources together with protection of land resources, as affected thereby.

E. The right to the use of water or to the flow of water in or from any natural stream, lake or other watercourse in this Commonwealth is and shall be limited to such water as may reasonably be required for the beneficial use of the public to be served; such right shall not extend to the waste or unreasonable use or unreasonable method of use of such water.

F. The quality of state waters is affected by the quantity of water and it is the intent of the Commonwealth, to the extent practicable, to maintain flow conditions to protect instream beneficial uses and public water supplies for human consumption.

§ 62.1-44.2. Short title; purpose.

The short title of this chapter is the State Water Control Law. It is the policy of the Commonwealth of Virginia and the purpose of this law to: (1) protect existing high quality state waters and restore all other state waters to such condition of quality that any such waters will permit all reasonable public uses and will support the propagation and growth of all aquatic life, including game fish, which might reasonably be expected to inhabit them; (2) safeguard the clean waters of the Commonwealth from pollution; (3) prevent any increase in pollution; (4) reduce existing pollution; (5) promote and encourage the reclamation and reuse of wastewater in a manner protective of the environment and public health; and (6) promote water resource conservation, management and distribution, and encourage water consumption reduction in order to provide for the health, safety, and welfare of the present and future citizens of the Commonwealth.

§ 62.1-44.3. (excerpt)

"State waters" means all water, on the surface and under the ground, wholly or partially within or bordering the Commonwealth or within its jurisdiction, including wetlands.

§62.1-194.1. Obstructing or contaminating state waters.

Except as otherwise permitted by law, it shall be unlawful for any person to dump, place or put, or cause to be dumped, placed or put into, upon the banks of or into the channels of any state waters any object or substance, noxious or otherwise, which may reasonably be expected to endanger, obstruct, impede, contaminate or substantially impair the lawful use or enjoyment of such waters and their environs by others.

VIRGINIA ADMINISTRATIVE CODE

24VAC30-73-90

E. Maintenance of private entrances shall be by the owner of the entrance, except that VDOT shall maintain:

1. On shoulder section highways, that portion of the entrance within the normal shoulder portion of the highway.

2. On highways with ditches, the drainage pipe at the entrance.

3. On highways with curb, gutter, and sidewalk belonging to VDOT, that portion of the entrance that extends to the back of the sidewalk. If a sidewalk is not present, that portion of the entrance that extends to the back of the curb line.

4. On highways with curb, gutter, and sidewalk not belonging to VDOT, only to the flow line of the gutter pan.

5. On highways with shoulders, ditches, and sidewalk belonging to VDOT, that portion of the entrance that extends to the back of the sidewalk.

Appendix C
National Hydrography Dataset

Technical and Other Details About the National Hydrography Dataset

The Memorandum of Understanding (MOU) between the Virginia Geographic Information Network (VGIN) and the Department of the Interior US Geological Survey (USGS) identifies what activities will be done to maintain high-resolution National Hydrography Dataset (NHD) and by which agency. The MOU applies only to the 1:24,000 scale NHD data. (The Environmental Protection Agency (EPA) is the steward for the medium resolution data (1:100,000 scale). The state stewards may provide information to the EPA, but do not maintain or revise the medium scale data directly.)

The NHD and WBD are digital vector datasets used by geographic information systems (GIS). These data are designed to be used in general mapping and in the analysis of surface water systems. In order to make a map these data must be used by a GIS to render the data and then print a map or make an image. The NHD is portrayed on the US Topo map product produced by the USGS and the NHD and WBD can be viewed on the Hydrography Viewer or the general mapping oriented The National Map Viewer.

In mapping, the NHD and WBD are used with other data themes such as elevation, boundaries, transportation, and structures to produce general reference maps. The NHD and WBD are often used by scientists using GIS. GIS technologies take advantage of a rich set of attributes imbedded in the data to generate specialized information. These analyses are possible because the NHD contains a flow network that allows for tracing water downstream or upstream. The NHD and WBD use an addressing system based on reach codes and linear referencing to link specific information about the water such as water discharge rates, water quality, and fish population downstream. (NHD.USGS.gov)

The WBD exists in six levels of a nested hierarchy permitting the analysis to determine which drainage basin a particular location is enclosed in. This makes it possible to determine which rivers and lakes could be affected by an event such as a toxic spill. Using basic NHD features like flow network, linked information, and other characteristics, along with one of the six levels of WBD areas, it is possible to study cause and effect relationships, such as how a source of poor water quality upstream might affect a fish population downstream. (nhd.usgs.gov)

The NHD is a large and comprehensive database. Building it required the cooperation of many government agencies at the Federal, state, and local level. These agencies banded together into a partnership to share data and resources, making it possible to complete nationwide coverage. The US Geological Survey played a key role in coordinating the partnership. Agencies such as the US Environmental Protection Agency, the US Department of Agriculture Forest Service, the US Department of Interior's National Park Service and Bureau of Land Management, along with state agencies played key roles in developing and building the NHD. These partnerships will remain intact to continue to maintain the NHD.

What is NHD Stewardship?

Just as building the NHD required a large partnership across the nation, maintaining the NHD also requires an extensive partnership, and can best be accomplished by those closest to the hydrography. Users within the states and federal lands understand the hydrography around them and are motivated to ensure the accuracy of the NHD to meet their business needs; therefore, they are ideally suited to become the stewards of the data; an agency in each state will manage the maintenance activities within the state. The maintenance will be performed by that agency or other agencies in the state. The United States Geological Survey (USGS) will facilitate the overall process, providing national management, coordination, tools, standards, documentation, training, quality assurance, data archival, and data distribution. Updates to the NHD will be made by the stewards, transmitted to the USGS, processed, and made available in the national dataset distribution. (http://nhd. usgs.gov/nhd_faq.html)

Information courtesy of US Department of the Interior, US Geological Survey and Commonwealth of Virginia.

Acknowledgments

Betsy Ripley introduced me to the people and culture of Mathews and welcomed me into her extended family, as did her sisters, Joanna Nix and Janice Phillips. Betsy's practical help and advice has been invaluable.

G.C. Morrow knows more about Mathews drainage than just about anyone on the planet. He identifies VDOT drainage failures and figures out the solutions. He understands Mathews: her people, their family histories, land and water. Thank you, G.C. for co-founding the Ditches of Mathews County project, sharing your knowledge and insights and encouraging me to finish this book when the task seemed overwhelming.

I am indebted to Janet Abbott Fast, owner of *Chesapeake Style* magazine, for her support and for providing the opportunity to share the Ditches of Mathews County story with the people of this region over the past two years.

David Arnold, Randy McFarland and Pete Modreski of the United State Geological Survey and Paul B. Moye, US Army Corps of Engineers, Norfolk District, your knowledge, courtesy and helpfulness are deeply appreciated, as are the efforts of David Malmquist, Dr. James E. Perry, III and Dr. Kimberly Reece of the Virginia Institute of Marine Science who went out of their way to investigate and identify the cyanobacteria in our ditches. Frankie Giles, Joe Williams and Joyce McGowan of VDOT and Lewie

Lawrence of MPPDC attempted to locate documents and provide answers whenever they could.

It would take another book to list everyone who helped make *Drowning a County* a reality, who shared information, background about Mathews and the impact of failed VDOT drainage here. Thank you to them and to the residents of Mathews who pulled over to see if I needed help when they saw my truck parked on the shoulder with the blinkers on while I photographed ditches or looked for cross pipes. Their concern is a reflection of the caring nature of this community.

I appreciate the efforts of those who helped locate and provide access to County records: Wendy Stewart, Treasurer;   Melinda Moran, Julie Kaylor, Deb Rhodes in Administration; John Shaw, Liz Whitley in Planning and Zoning, Bette Dillehay, Library Director; and the very special women of the County Clerk's Office: Angela Ingram, Judy Dixon and Daria Linsinbigler.

I am grateful to Karyn Austin, Kate Bunner, Davie Cottrell, David and Jamie Davis, Jackie Guidry, C.L. Howland, Cheryl Hugo, Ruth Litschewski, Lynne Pryde and Elena Siddall for their support and thoughtful comments on the manuscript.

To the person closest to my heart, John Doppler, my son and fellow writer, who taught me how to cope with the intricacies of Scrivener, created the cover art and handled the book design and typesetting, thank you. No mother could be prouder of her son than I am of you and of what a remarkable and talented man you are.

Thank you to each one I've cited here, and to everyone who made this come-here feel she came home to Mathews.

Glossary

accrete to grow by accumulation

accretion a gradual process where layers of a material are formed as small amounts are added

aggradation increase in land elevation through the deposit of sediment

anoxic lack of oxygen

aquifer a zone of saturation; an underground layer of water-bearing permeable rock or materials from which groundwater can be extracted using a water well (USGS)

barrier beach a sand ridge that runs parallel to the shore

barrier island accumulations of sand that are separated from the mainland by open water

berm a raised area or bank

biofiltration a technique using living material to slow stormwater flow and filter out sediment or oily materials

bioretention the process of capturing and holding stormwater to concentrate and remove contaminants from stormwater runoff

BMAA (beta-N-methlyamino-L-alanine) an amino acid produced by cyanobacteria, which studies have linked to Alzheimer's Disease, Lewie Body Dementia, Lou Gehrig's Disease (ALS) and Parkinson's in genetically susceptible individuals

BMP (Best Management Practice) a method or technique selected as the most effective to achieve a goal

brine water saturated with salt

Byrd Act; Byrd Road Act 1932 legislation to help Virginia counties after the Great Depression of 1929 where the state took over responsibility and control of the secondary road system

channelized stream the practice of directing a stream's flow under a road through pipes or culverts

chlorides salts of sodium (NaCl), potassium (KCl) or calcium (CaCl2)

Clean Water Act legislation to regulate discharges of pollutants into waters of the United States and set quality standards for all contaminants in surface waters (33 U.S.C. §1251)

confining layer a layer of dense material in the ground that water cannot penetrate, such as granite or clay

conveyance the action of transporting something from one place to another

cross pipe a pipe that carries stormwater from one side of a road to the other

CSO combined sewer overflow; a combined sewer carries stormwater runoff, domestic sewage and industrial wastewater in the same pipe

culvert a structure that allows water to flow under a road; may be a pipe or a concrete structure

cyanobacteria formerly known as blue-green algae, these are bacteria that use photosynthesis for energy, and use sunlight like plants to manufacture their own food; primarily live in still water, but can survive in moist soil as well

cyanotoxins harmful chemicals produced by cyanobacteria

cytotoxin a substance that has a harmful effect on certain cells

deed a legal document conveying or transfering property or rights

dermatotoxin a harmful substance that affects skin

detention pond an area designed to temporarily hold and slow down the flow of stormwater moving to another area and allow some infiltration into the soil

ditch a narrow channel dug in the ground for drainage

ditch bank the side walls of a ditch

ditch enhancement a bioretention system used in Washington State (See http://www.kitsapgov.com/sswm/pdf/Kitsap_Roadside _Ditch_WQ_Enhancement_Plan.pdf)

easement a right to cross or use someone else's land for a specified purpose

ecosystem a community of living things interacting within their environment as a unit

elevation height of land above sea level

ephemeral stream a usually dry area that flows as a stream only during part of the year, usually after rainfall or when the water table is high

eutrophication a condition where water receives excess nitrogen and/or phosphorus that stimulates plant growth and cyanobacterial growth

evapotranspiration loss of water from soil and bodies of water by evaporation and/or movement through a plant and evaporation from its leaves

factoid a statement that has no basis in fact, but is reported in print and repeated so often it becomes accepted as a fact; invented by Norman Mailer in his biography, *Marilyn*

flow line a line on a map indicating the general path water takes as it moves

green infrastructure stormwater management systems that mimic nature by soaking up and storing water (EPA)

groundwater water that seeps down through the soil, filling spaces between rock particles

growing season the period of time in the year when plant growth takes place

hardscape the built environment or landscape; includes streets, sidewalks, structures, walls, parking lots, wooden decks, etc.

hepatotoxin a harmful substance that damages liver tissue

hydraulics the principles governing water or other liquids in action

hydrology the science of the occurrence, distribution, movement and properties of the waters of the earth (USGS)

impact crater the depression caused by a meteor strike (35 million years ago one led to the formation of the Chesapeake Bay; the roughly circular crater is more than 50 miles wide and .8 mi deep)

impermeable not allowing water to pass through

impervious not allowing water to pass through

infiltration water flow through small openings or pores (USGS)

iRUMS 2003 RUMS migrated from a client-server situation to the VDOT intranet as iRUMS (VDOT)

intermittent stream a stream that usually only flows in the rainy season and is dry at other times of the year

jetty a pier or structure extending into the sea or other body of water to protect a harbor, a channel, a pier, etc., or to deflect the current

LIDAR (Light Detection and Ranging) a remote sensing technology that collects 3-dimentional point clouds of the Earth's surface (USGS)

linear project structures built in a straight line, like roads, ditches, canals, tunnels

littoral drift the process of sand and sediment moved by wind and wave action hitting the shoreline at an angle; same as longshore transport

longshore transport the process of sand and sediment moved by wind and wave action hitting the shoreline at an angle; same as littoral drift

mean sea level a reference point used to measure elevation

microcystins a toxic chemical released by cyanobacteria when they die or their cell walls are ruptured; named for one type of cyanobacteria, Microcystis aeruginosa, microcystins are found in other species as well

MSL see Mean Sea Level

National Hydrography Dataset the surface-water component of The National Map using common features such as lakes, ponds, streams, rivers, canals, streamgages, and dams. (USGS)

National Map a map containing aerial photographs, elevation, geographic names, hydrography, boundaries, transportation, structures, and land cover for the entire country (USGS)

neurotoxin a substance harmful to nerves or nerve tissue

NHD see National Hydrography Dataset

outfall ditch a man-made or channelized natural stream carrying stormwater from VDOT roadside ditches to a receiving body of water (a creek, river or bay)

oxic containing oxygen

pollutant a substance with undesirable impacts

pollutant loading reduction a way to lower the concentration of an undesirable substance in air or water

post-glacial rebound a change in the shape of the Earth related to the withdrawal/melting of ice sheets from the last glacial period

potable water that's safe to drink

pre-development hydrology the natural flow of water in a watershed before humans built roads and other structures

prescriptive easement a public road pursuant to § 33.1-184, which provides that:

When a way has been regularly or periodically worked by road officials as a public road and used by the public as such continuously for a period of twenty years, proof of these facts shall be conclusive evidence that the same is a public road. In all such cases the center of the general line of passage, conforming to the ancient landmarks where such exist, shall be presumed to be the center of the way and in the absence of proof to the contrary the width shall be presumed to be thirty feet.

retention pond an area designed to hold stormwater and only allow it to overflow when the pond reaches a certain capacity

revenue sharing a program that allows a county to provide 50% of the funding for a desired transportation project which will be matched with state funds

rhizome the thickened root structure of certain plants which absorbs and holds nutrients

right-of-way a type of easement granted over land for transportation purposes or utility use

rotoditching using an earthmoving machine that cuts a channel with a rounded bottom and relatively straight sides

RUMS Right of Way and Utility Management System: a 1999, $2.5 million software program to track right-of-way transactions and project schedules.

runoff movement of precipitation along the ground after it falls

sea level rise, global the rate of increase in the average height of all the world's oceans (NOAA)

sea level rise, relative average increase in coastal water height measured relative to a specific point on land (NOAA)

sediment transport movement of silt, sand, clay or soil carried by stormwater flow

semi-empirical sea level rise model a computer model that connects global sea level rise to global mean surface temperature (Rahmstorf 2007.)

slope the direction and steepness of a line

storm drain a below-ground system of pipes and channels that carry stormwater

subsidence the sinking of a land mass

surficial related to the surface of something; surficial water table is the water table near the surface of the land

surficial aquifer a shallow aquifer usually less than 50 feet beneath the surface of the land

swale water-harvesting ditches that are generally wide and flat

swamp a forested wetland

tidal related to the periodic rise and fall of a body of water caused by the gravitation influence between the Sun, Moon and the Earth (NOAA)

tidal marsh coastal wetland with salt-tolerant herbs, grasses and shrubs that protects the coastline

tide gate a structure that allows water to flow in one direction of the tide and closes in the other

tide gauge a device to measure and track the change in sea level at a specific location

TMDL (Total Maximum Daily Load) the amount of a contaminant calculated to be the highest amount a body of water can tolerate without exceeding pollution limits

topo (topographic map) a map with contours of the elevation of the area shown

topography science of land shape and features

toxin poisonous or venomous substance

underdrain a structure under a road or stormwater management device to allow excess water to move away

upland an area uphill at a higher elevation from a lower area

state waters "all waters, on the surface and under the ground, wholly or partially within or bordering the Commonwealth or within its jurisdiction and which affect the public welfare;" defined in Code of Virginia Title 62.1-10.

watershed an area of land that drains all the streams and rainfall to a common outlet such as the mouth of a bay or any point along a stream channel

water table the upper surface of a zone of saturation (USGS); the top level of the aquifer closest to the surface

References

Batzer, Donald P. and Rebecca P. Sharitz, eds. *Ecology of Freshwater and Estuarine Wetlands*. Berkeley, California: University of California Press. 2007. Print.

Bova, Carol J. *Inside the Crater*. Blog. 2012-2014. [http://insidethecrater.com]

-------- "The Ditches of Mathews County." 2012-2014. *Chesapeake Style Magazine*. Print/Web.

Brennan, F.P., V. O'Flaherty, G. Kramers, J. Grant and K.G. Richards. "Long-term persistence and leaching of Escherichia coli in temperate maritime soils." *Applied Environmental Microbiology*. Mar 2010:76(5):1449-1455. Web. 14 Aug. 2014.

Churro, Catarina, Elsa Dias and Elisabete Valério. "Risk Assessment of Cyanobacteria and Cyanotoxins, the Particularities and Challenges of *Planktothrix spp*. Monitoring." *Novel Approaches and Their Applications in Risk Assessment*. Ed. Yuzhou Luo. InTech. 2012: 59-84. Web. 5 July 2014. [http://cdn. intechopen.com/pdfs/35502.pdf].

City of Norfolk, Virginia - Official Website. *About Us*. n.d. Web. 5 July 2014.

Clifford, Candace. *New Point Comfort Light Station Historical Documentation*. 3:4; 39:40. Mathews County Historical Society. 2001. Web. 5 July 2014

Coder, Kim. D. "Flood Damage to Trees." *University of Georgia School of Forest Resources Extension Publication for 94-601*. July 1994. Web 13 Aug. 2014.

Cole, Wanda Diane. *Sea Level Rise: Technical Guidance for Dorchester County*. 2008. Maryland Department of Natural Resources. Chesapeake and Coastal Management Program. Web. 4 July 2014.

Commonwealth of Virginia. *Review of the Virginia Department of Transportation's GASB Infrastructure Valuation*. 2000. Office of the Auditor of Public Accounts. Web. 5 July 2014.

Commonwealth of Virginia. Commonwealth Transportation Board. *Meetings and Agendas 1920-2014*. Web. 5 July 2014.

Commonwealth of Virginia. Department of Environmental Quality. *Appendix 1 Integrated List of All Waters*. 2012. Web. 5 July 2014.

-------- *Final TMDL Implementation Plans: Piankatank River, Gwynns Island, Milford Haven Implementation Plan*. 2013. Web. 5 July 2014.

-------- *Guidance Memorandum No. 08-2004: Regulation of Ditches under the Virginia Water Protection Permit Program*. 13 May 2008. Web. 18 July 2014.

-------- "What's Local Governments [*sic*] Role in Climate Change?" Middle Peninsula Planning District Commission. 2010. Web. 15 Aug. 2014.

Commonwealth of Virginia. Department of Health. *Eastern Equine Encephalitis (EEE) Fact Sheet*. 29 March 2013. Web. 18 July 2014.

Commonwealth of Virginia. Department of Highways. "Map of Mathews County showing Primary and Secondary Highways 58-35, 1932 revised 1935." *Official County Highway Maps*. n.d. Virginia Surveyors Foundation. CD.

Commonwealth of Virginia. Department of Transportation. *A History of Roads in Virginia, "The Most Convenient Wayes," Special Centennial Edition*. 2006. Web. 6 July 2014.

-------- *ANNUAL REPORT 2013 Pursuant to: Chapters 36 and 152 of the 2011 Acts of Assembly of the Virginia General Assembly*. Web. 30 Nov. 2013. 3 Oct. 2014.

-------- *Biennial Report on the Condition of and Investment Needed to Maintain and Operate the Existing Surface Transportation Infrastructure for FY 2011 and FY 2012*. Web. 2009. 18 July 2014.

-------- *Board of Supervisors Manual*. Web. 2012. 18 July 2014. [http://www.virginiadot.org/business/resources/local_assistance/BOS_Manual_-_2012_update.pdf]

-------- *Daily Traffic Volume Estimates Jurisdiction Report 57 Mathews County*. Web. 2012. 18 July 2014. [http://www.virginiadot.org/info/2011_traffic_data_by_jurisdiction.asp.]

-------- *Drainage Manual*. 2002 Rev. 2014. Web. 18 July 2014. [http://www.virginiadot.org/business/resources/LocDes/DrainageManual/START_VDOT_Drainage_Manual.pdf].

-------- *Maintenance Best Practices*. 68:73. VDOT FOIA Correspondence. 02 Feb. 2012.

-------- *Mileage Tables 1998-2012*. 31 Jan. 2014. Web. 30 July 2014.

-------- *Pavement Design Guide for Subdivision and Secondary Roads in Virginia*. Revised 2009. Web. 19 July 2014.

-------- *Report on the Condition of and Investment Needed to Maintain and Operate the Existing Surface Transportation Infrastructure for FY 2013 and 2014*. 2011. Web. 19 July 2014.

-------- *Right of Way Manual of Instructions*. 2011. Web. 19 July 2014.

-------- *Rural Rustic Road Program Manual*. 2011. Web. 19 July 2014.

-------- *State of the Pavement 2012*. 2012. Web. 19 July 2014.

-------- *State Highway Plat Books. 1-4*. 1950-2014. Collection of state road plan sheets. (Located Mathews County Courthouse Records Room.)

Commonwealth of Virginia. Joint Legislative Audit and Review Commission of the Virginia General Assembly. *Adequacy and Management of VDOT's Highway Maintenance Program*. 2001. Web. 19 July 2014.

Commonwealth of Virginia. State Water Control Board. Siudyla, E. A.; Berglund, T. D. and Newton, V. P. and Tidewater Regional Office. Bureau of Water Control Management. "Groundwater of the Middle Peninsula, Virginia." *Planning Bulletin 305*. 1977. Web. 5 July 2014.

Commonwealth of Virginia. Virginia Marine Resources Commission. *Subaqueous Guidelines*. VMRC Regulations. March 1986 updated November 2005. Web. 31 July, 2014.

Ditches of Mathews County Facebook Page. 2012-2014. Web. [www.facebook.com/MCditches]

Draper Aden Associates. *Services*. Web. 14 Aug. 2014. [http://www.daa.com/services]

Eggleston, Jack, and Jason Pope. "Land subsidence and relative sea-level rise in the southern Chesapeake Bay region." *U.S. Geological Survey Circular 1392*. 2013. Web. 15 Aug. 2014.

Glick, Patty; Jonathan Clough, Brad Nunley. *Sea-Level Rise and Coastal Habitats in the Chesapeake Bay Region*. National Wildlife Federation. Technical Report. 2008. Web. 5 July 2014.

Hansen, Dennis L., John J. Clark, Satoshi Ishii, Michael J. Sadowsky and Randall E. Hicks. "Sources and Sinks of *Escherichia coli* in Benthic and Pelagic Fish." *Journal Great Lakes Research*. 34:228-234. International Association for Great Lakes Research. 2008. Web. 21 July 2014.

Hardaway, C.S., Jr., et al. *New Point Comfort Lighthouse Mathews, Virginia Site Assessment Report*. Gloucester Point, Virginia. Virginia Institute of Marine Science. 2008. Web. 6 July 2014.

Hardaway, C.S., Jr., D.A. Milligan, L.M. Varnell, C.A. Wilcox, G.R. Thomas. *Shoreline Evolution Chesapeake Bay and Piankatank River Shorelines Mathews County, Virginia*. Gloucester Point, Virginia. Virginia Institute of Marine Science. 2005. Web. 19 July 2014.

Hardaway, C.S., Jr., D.A. Milligan, C.H. Hobbs, C.A. Wilcox, K.P. O'Brien, L. Varnell. *Mathews County Shoreline Management Plan*. Special Report in Applied Marine Science and Ocean Engineering, No. 417. Gloucester Point, Virginia. Virginia Institute of Marine Science. 2010. Web. 25 July 2014.

Harding, William R. *A Research Strategy for the Detection and Management of Algal Toxins in Water Sources*. Water Resource Commission. June, 2006. Web. 15 Apr. 2014.

Hicks, R.E., S. Ishii, D.L. Hansen, M.J. Sadowsky, T. Yan, H. Vu. "Factors controlling long-term survival and growth of naturalized Escherichia coli populations in temperate soils." *Microbes and Environments*. 2010;25(1)8-14. Web. 20 July 2014.

Hobbs, C.H., G.L. Anderson, R.J. Byrne, J.M. Zeigler. *Mathews County Shoreline Situation Report*. Gloucester Point, Virginia. Virginia Institute of Marine Science. 1975. Web. 6 July 2014.

Holst, Thomas, Niels Jørgensen, Claus Jørgensen, Anders Johansen. "Degradation of microcystin in sediments at oxic and anoxic, denitfying conditions." *Water Research*. November 2003. 37(19):4748-4760. Web. 18 July 2014.

Holtcamp, Wendee. "The Emerging Science of BMAA: Do Cyanobacteria
    Contribute to Neurodegenerative Disease?" Mar 2012 120(3): a110–a116.
    Environmental Health Perspectives.Web. 6 July 2014.

Jevrejeva, Woodworth and Brewer. "Comments on "A Semi-Empirical Approach to
    Projecting Future Sea Level Rise," *Science*. 317:5846. 28 Sept. 2007: 1866. Web.
    5 July 2014.

Kashian, Donna, Vijay Kannappan, Hunter Oakes, Carly Collins. *Multiple Stressors
    PI Research*. Wayne State University. 2010. Experimental work. Web. 20 July
    2014. [http://www.glerl.noaa.gov/res/projects/multi_stressors/restricted/2011/
    Multi-Stress2011%20Donna%20Kashian.ppt]

Mailer, Norman. *Marilyn*: A Biography. 1973. Location 125. Polaris
    Communications and the Norman Mailer Estate. Electronic book, 2011.

Mathews County, Virginia. *Board of Supervisors Minutes 2008-2014*. Web. 5 July
    2014. [County website:Meeting Portal.]

--------- *Land Records*. Web. 5 July 2014.

--------- For Residents. *2030 Comprehensive Plan*. 2010. Web. 5 July 2014.

--------- Planning, Zoning & Wetlands. *2030 Comprehensive Plan Appendix*. 2010.
    Web. 5 July 2014.

Mathews County, Virginia. *Board of Supervisors Minutes, 1933-2007*. Mathews,
    Virginia. Minutes Books. [Clerk of Circuit Court. Liberty Square Courthouse;
    County Administration, Historic Courthouse Complex]

McFarland, E. Randolph and T. Scott Bruce. *The Virginia Coastal Plain
    Hydrogeologic Framework*. Reston, VA. U. S. Geological Survey. 2006. Web. 19
    July 2014. (Professional Paper: 1731.)

Meneely, J.P., C.T. Elliot. "Microcystins: measuring human exposure and the impact
    on human health." *Biomarkers*. 2013 Dec;18(8):639-49. Web. 19 July 2014.

Middle Peninsula Planning District Commission. *Meeting Minutes 1968-2011*.
    Saluda, Virginia. MPPDC Library.

-------- Shore Engineering. *Drainage Study of the Garden Creek Area*. Saluda,
    Virginia. 1980. Print. (Copy located Mathews County Planning and Zoning
    Office.)

-------- *Water Supply Management on the Middle Peninsula of Virginia—An Information Review*. Saluda, Virginia. Middle Peninsula Planning District Commission. 2002. Print.

-------- *Past Meeting Packets FY 2012-2014*. Web. 5 July 2014.

-------- *Assessing the economic and ecological impacts of sea level rise for select vulnerable locations within the Middle Peninsula*. 2009. Web. 5 July 2014.

-------- *Middle Peninsula Climate Change Adaptation—An assessment of potential Anthropogenic and Ecological Impacts of Climate Change on the Peninsula-Phase I*. 2009. Web. 5 July 2014.

-------- *Middle Peninsula Climate Change Adaptation: Facilitation of Presentations and Discussions of Climate Change Issues with Local Elected Officials and the General Public—Phase 2*. 2010. Web. 5 July 2014.

-------- *Initiating Adaptation Public Policy Development Phase 3*. 2012. Web. 5 July 2014.

-------- John S. Morris, III. *Roadside and Outfall Drainage Ditches*. 2013. Middle Peninsula Planning District Commission Report. Web. 5 July 2013.

-------- "1980's Major MPPDC Accomplishments." Saluda, Virginia. Middle Peninsula Planning District Commission. Web. 26 July 2014. [http://www.mppdc.com/index.php/40-years]

National Center for Environmental Health, Div. of Emergency and Environmental Health Services. *Stormwater Management and Vector Breeding Habitats*. CDC. June 2012. Web. 3 July 2014.

National Oceanic and Atmospheric Administration, Office of Coast Survey. "Navigation Chart of the Chesapeake Bay." 1872. Nautical Chart. Web. 5 Aug. 2014.

-------- "Chesapeake Bay, Mobjack Bay and York River Entrance." Nautical Chart 12238. 2009. Web. 5 Aug. 2014.

New Point Comfort Lighthouse History. n.d. NewPointComfort.com. Web. 15 Aug. 2014.

Oberholster, PJ, A-M Botha and JU Grobbelaar. "Microcystis aeruginosa: source of toxic microcystins in drinking water." *African Journal of Biotechnology*. 2004, Mar; 3:159-168. Web. 31 July 2014.

Peng, Yilang. "Arboretum Wetlands Releasing Rather than Treating Harmful Nutrients." *Madison Commons*. 30 June 2013. Web. 27 July 2014. [http://madisoncommons.org]

Pyke, C. R., R.G. Najjar, M.B. Adams, D. Breitburg, M. Kemp, C. Hershner, R. Howarth, M. Mulholland, M. Paolisso, D. Secor, K. Sellner, D. Wardrop, and R. Wood. *Climate Change and the Chesapeake Bay: State-of-the-Science Review and Recommendations*. Annapolis, MD. Chesapeake Bay Program Science and Technical Advisory Committee (STAC). 2008. Web. 5 July 2014.

Powars, D. S., T. S. Bruce. "The Effects of the Chesapeake Bay Impact Crater on the Geological Framework and Correlation of Hydrogeologic Units of the Lower York-James Peninsula, Virginia." Professional Paper 1612. United States Geological Survey. 2000. Web. 5 July 2014.

Powars, D. S. "The Effects of the Chesapeake Bay Impact Crater on the Geologic Framework and the Correlation of Hydrogeologic Units of Southeastern Virginia, South of the James River." USGS Professional Paper 1622. 2000.

Qiu, Jane. "China Cuts Methane Emissions from Rice Fields." *Nature*. 2009. Web. 7 July 2014.

Rahmstorf, Stefan. "A Semi-Empirical Approach to Projecting Future Sea-Level Rise." *Science* 19 January 2007: 368-370. Web. 5 July 2014.

Schmith, Johansen, Thejll and Holgate. "Comments on "A Semi-Empirical Approach to Projecting Future Sea Level Rise," *Science*. 317:5846. 28 September 2007: 1866. Web. 5 July 2014.

Schwartz, Rick. *Hurricanes and the Middle Atlantic States*. Alexandria, Virginia. Blue Diamond Books. 2007. Print.

Semenov, A.V., L. van Overbeek, A.J. Termorshuizen, A.H. van Bruggen. "Influence of aerobic and anaerobic conditions on survival of Escherichia coli O157:H7 and Salmonella enterica serovar Typhimurium in Luria-Bertani broth, farm-yard manure and slurry." *Journal of Environmental Management*. March 2011; Epub 2010 Oct. 28.

Snead, Sande. "RUMS Right-of-Way Tracking." *Public Roads*. Vol. 68 · No. 4. United States Department of Transportation Federal Highway Administration. Jan/Feb 2005. Web. 17 July 2014. [https://www.fhwa.dot.gov/publications/publicroads/05jan/04.cfm].

United States Army Corps of Engineers. *The Secretary of the Army Transmitting A Letter from the Chief of Engineers, Department of the Army, dated November 29, 1963, Submitting a Report, Together with Accompanying Papers and Illustrations, on an Interim Hurricane Survey of Garden Creek, Mathews, County, Virginia.* House Document No. 216, 88th Congress, 2nd Session. Print.

-------- Office of the District Engineer. *Hurricane Survey Chesapeake Bay, Potomac and Rappahannock Rivers, Appraisal Report.* Washington District, Washington D.C. June 1956. Web. 6 July 2014.

United States Census Bureau. 1910 Census; 2000 Census; 2010 Census. Web. 5 July 2014.

United States. Center for Global Health, Div. of Parasitic Diseases and Malaria. *Raccoon Latrines: Identification and Clean-up.* n.d. Web. 5 July 2014.

United States. Centers for Disease Control and Prevention. *Chikungunya Virus.* 2 July 2014. Web. 14 Aug. 2014.

-------- *Eastern Equine Encephalitis.* 16 Aug. 2010. Web. 5 July 2014.

United States. Department of Agriculture. Forest Service. *Silvics of North America.* Agriculture Handbook 654, Volume 1: Conifers. *Pinus taeda L.* 1990. Web. July 2014.

United States. Department of Agriculture. NASS. *Census of Agriculture: 1910; 2007; 2012.* Web. 5 July 2014.

United States. Department of Agriculture. Soil Conservation Service. *Soil Survey of Mathews County, Virginia.* Series 1958, No. 24. Issued November 1962. Print.

United States. Department of Transportation Federal Highway Administration. *Geotechnical Aspects of Pavements Reference Manual.* NHI-05-037. Ch. 7. 2006. Web. 7 July 2014.

United States. Environmental Protection Agency. *Summary of the Clean Water Act 33 U.S.C. §1251 et seq. (1972).* Web. 5 July 2014.

-------- *Storm Water Technology Fact Sheet Bioretention.* 1999. Web. 30 June 2014.

United States. Environmental Protection Agency Office of Air and Radiation. "Coastal Elevations and Sensitivity to Sea Level Rise." *Background Documents Supporting Climate Change Science Program Synthesis and Assessment Product 4.1.* Eds. J.G. Titus and E.M. Strange. EPA 430R07004. Washington, D. C. 2008. Web. 6 July 2014.

United States. Federal Emergency Management Agency. *2013 FEMA Flood Information Portal for Region III.* 2013. Web. [http://www.maps.riskmap3.com/VA]. 14 Aug. 2014

-------- *2013 FEMA Preliminary Coastal Study.* 2013 Web. [http://www.fema.gov/national-flood-insurance-program-flood-hazard-mapping]. 14 Aug. 2014.

-------- *Floodplain Management—Principles and Current Practices.* EMI FEMA Training Guide. 8-1; 9-2. Web. 30 July 2014. [http://training.fema.gov/EMIweb/edu/fmpcp.asp]

United States Geological Survey. *Carbon Storage in U.S. Eastern Ecosystems Helps Counter Greenhouse Gas Emissions.* Released: June 25, 2014. *USGS Newsroom.*

-------- *Historical Topographic Map Collection (HTMC).* Web. 7 July 2014. [http://nationalmap.gov/historical/]

Vega-Rua, A; Zouache, K; Girdo, R; Failloux, AB; Lourenco-de-Oliveira, R. "High Level of Vector Competence of Aedes aegypti and Aedes albopictus From Ten American Countries as a Crucial Factor in the Spread of Chikungunya Virus." *Journal of Virology.* June 2014. Web. 5 July 2014.

Zedler, J.B. *How Hydrologic Manipulations Can Accelerate Cattail Invasions via "Internal Eutrophication."* University of Wisconsin-Madison. Arboretum Leaflet 7. Web. 21 July 2014. [http://uwarboretum.org/publications/leaflets/index_3.php]

-------- *How Ponded Runoff and Invasive Cattails Reduced Wetland Ecosystem Services in Three Experimental Wetlands.* University of Wisconsin Arboretum. Leaflet #27. 2013. Web. 14 Aug. 2014. [http://uwarboretum.org/publications/leaflets/PDF/Leaflet27.pdf]

-------- *How Ponded Cattail Marshes Can Export Phosphorus: A Conceptual Model.* University of Wisconsin Arboretum. Leaflet #28. 2013. Web. 21 July 2014. [http://uwarboretum.org/publications/leaflets/PDF/Leaflet28.pdf]

Zervas, C.E. *Sea Level Variations of the United States 1854-1999*. 2001. Silver
    Spring, MD.: U.S. Dept. of Commerce, National Oceanic and Atmospheric
    Administration, National Ocean Service. (Technical Report NOS CO-OPS 36).
    Web. 19 July 2014.

-------- *Sea Level Variations of the United States 1854-2006*. 2009. Silver Spring, MD.
    U.S. Dept. of Commerce, National Oceanic and Atmospheric Administration,
    National Ocean Service. (Technical Report NOS CO-OPS 53). Web. 19 July
    2014.

Index

About The Author

Photo by Deborah Figg

Carol J. Bova found a new lifestyle as a writer in 2004 after moving from California to Mathews, Virginia, a rural Chesapeake Bay peninsula. In January 2012, she and G.C. Morrow co-founded the Ditches of Mathews County, a grass-roots volunteer project, to investigate and offer information to the Virginia Department of Transportation to help resolve highway drainage issues impacting landowners. When her research uncovered a history of VDOT-created myths used to avoid basic ditch maintenance for decades, Carol began compiling the information used in *Drowning a County*.

In 2012-13, Carol served on the Steering Committee for the Piankatank, Milford Haven, Gwynns Island Water Quality Improvement Plan approved by the U.S. Environmental Protection Agency in August 2014. The Ditches of Mathews County was a community partner in the development of that clean-up plan. The US Geological Survey accepted Carol's July 2014 request to correct the flow lines on *The National Map* Hydrography Dataset for Garden Creek and the breach in the Winter Harbor barrier beach.

Carol is a columnist for *Chesapeake Style* magazine, a novelist and the President of the Chesapeake Bay Writers chapter of the Virginia Writers Club. When not researching or writing, Carol enjoys photography, genealogy and creating silver jewelry. Carol shares her home with William the Cat, who found her at the Gloucester-Mathews Humane Society.

16869311R00124

Made in the USA
Middletown, DE
23 December 2014